A FEAST OF FESTIVALS

And I said to the man who stood at the gate of the year: 'Give me a light that I may tread safely into the unknown.' And he replied: 'Go out into the darkness and put your hand into the hand of God. That shall be better to you than light and safer than a known way.'

Minnie Louise Haskins 1875 — 1957

A FEAST OF FESTIVALS

Celebrating the spiritual seasons of the year

HUGO SLIM

Marshall Pickering
An Imprint of HarperCollinsPublishers

To my mother, Buffy Slim

Marshall Pickering is an Imprint of
HarperCollins*Religious*
Part of HarperCollins*Publishers*
77–85 Fulham Palace Road, London W6 8JB

First published in Great Britain
in 1996 by Marshall Pickering

1 3 5 7 9 10 8 6 4 2

A catalogue record for this book is
available from the British Library

0 551 02850-5

Printed and bound in Great Britain by
HarperCollinsManufacturing Glasgow

Acknowledgements

Several people have given me valuable practical help and moral support during the writing of this book. Cristina Odone, David Bodanis and Catherine Clarke helped in various ways to get me started. Sarah and Robert Whyte gave me a wonderful place to write in Somerset, and Neville and Dizzy Spinney provided a similar haven in Suffolk. My particular thanks for their comments and suggestions go to Helen Marshall, David Barlow, Marc and Rachel Polonsky, and my editor Christine Smith. Special thanks also go to Margaret Stoton for childminding over a hot summer so I could meet my deadline. My greatest thanks of all go to my wife Becky for her unfailing encouragement and advice at every stage of the book, and to my little daughter Jessica who was born on All Saints' Day 1994 and has grown together with this book. By making me so happy they have been a constant inspiration.

Oxford
All Saints Day 1995

A NOTE ON BIBLE READINGS AND SOURCES

The various readings from the gospels given in the text are taken from the Church of England's Alternative Service Book (ASB). For most Sundays and some festivals, a choice of readings is given. In this case, the first reading is the reading for Year 1 and the second is the reading for Year 2. Different Churches will obviously follow different service books and lectionaries and may find these readings at odds with their own. However, for the purposes of this book, I felt it better to stick to one set of readings for the whole year.

Many sources have been useful to me while researching this book, but some deserve special mention and might be of interest as further reading. F. X. Weiser spent many years researching the origins and rituals of Christian festivals. His findings were very helpful in writing this book and are presented in his delightful book *A Handbook of Christian Feasts and Customs*, published in 1958.

Two modern books might appeal more to today's reader. Marian Green's *A Calendar of Festivals* is a lively summary of the pre-Christian roots of many of today's festivals, while David Self's book *High Days and Holidays* is an excellent introduction to the Christian Year for children.

Contents

The End of the Year   189

APPENDICES

Introduction

For everything there is a season,
and a time for every matter under heaven.

Ecclesiastes 3:1

This is a book for anyone who wishes to know more about the main festivals and holy days of the Christian faith, their origins and meaning, when they occur, and how they are celebrated. It explains how the events of Christ's life coincide with the seasons of nature to shape the Christian Year. Appropriate Biblical readings for each season and festival are given alongside the text so that the book can be a practical companion to both private meditation and public worship throughout the year. There is also some reflection on each season and its festivals so that the reader can see how they fit together to make up the sacred calendar.

A SENSE OF TIME

People are obsessed with time these days. We live by our watches and are seldom out of sight of a clock. Even our church services are frequently interrupted by the irritating squeak of somebody's digital watch telling him or her that it is time to do something else. A friend of mine recently told me that when the clocks move forwards or backwards in spring and autumn, he not only has to change the time on his wrist watch, but has to traipse around the house adjusting the clocks on twelve other electronic contraptions.

His video has a clock on it, his oven has a clock, and even a new iron he had ordered turned up with a small digital clock on it.

The time with which we are obsessed is clock time. Our lives are ruled, terrorized even, by the hours, minutes and seconds around which we have chosen to organize our days. But clock time is not a very relaxed form of time. One of the most stressful periods of my life was when I spent two years commuting to London by train every day. The timing of my working day was an extremely tense affair, rigidly suspended between the 07.52 train in the morning and the 18.20 in the evening. In order not to miss these two pivotal moments in my day, I had to develop a split-second routine which had me tearing around between bedroom and bathroom, bus stop and station, office and underground station.

Like millions of others, I had soon programmed myself quite effectively and had my journey and its timing down to a fine art. But all the time I had a sense of being enslaved to a rhythm that was not my own, and one which seemed relentlessly and inhumanly monotonous. The vast majority of days were exactly the same. The only thing which changed was the countryside outside the carriage window. While my days were endlessly repetitious, the landscape changed from winter to spring, from summer to autumn. The changing seasons kept my spirits up and reminded me that the time I kept was not the only time there is.

FROM CLOCK TIME TO GOD'S TIME

As part of God's creation, human beings have always lived with time and the cycles and seasons of the natural world. Into these cycles people have woven the pattern of a religious calendar which commemorates their experience and understanding of God. Sadly, many of the traditional landmarks of the Christian Year have been lost in today's industrial and post-industrial world. The sacred days and weeks that once gave structure and meaning to the year beyond the mere passing of time are now only faintly observed. Their significance is more commercial than religious. For the majority of people, living and working in the bustle of big cities, time is divided into long months of work and a few weeks of holiday. The major Christian festivals have simply become short breaks in the working year, and many lesser festivals are now largely unknown.

But a sense of ritual time is essential to the human soul. Rediscovering and enjoying the seasons and festivals of the sacred calendar frees a part of us to live beyond clock time. It puts us in touch with a sense of time which concerns the mood and movements of our soul and not just the dates and timings of our diary. This sense of time is perhaps best described as soul time or God's time. It has been long nurtured in the Christian calendar, the shape and structure of which has been developed over hundreds of years. The Christian Year – God's time – combines the recurring miracles of the agricultural calendar with the eternal mysteries of God's revelation of Himself in the life, death and resurrection of Christ. By living these mysteries anew each year in the seasons and festivals of the Christian calendar, we

can feel the steady pulse of God's grace and purpose behind the different seasons. Experiencing the Christian
Year's high points and low points, its light and its darkness,
gives texture, rhythm and meaning to the passing of time.
It frees us from the dreadful rush and sameness of clock
time in the modern world – a world in which time itself is in
danger of becoming banal.

JOURNEYING THROUGH THE CHRISTIAN YEAR

The beginning of every year is like the beginning of a journey. The human soul is naturally restless, and one of the
most common images of faith is as a calling and a journey.
Something stirs in the hearts of people like Abraham or
Bunyan's Christian, and they uproot themselves and go in
search of it. Yet there is also a part of the soul which recognizes that it is already at home in God, and has no need of
journeys.

The creativity of our religious life lies in this tension between the still and the moving, the homestead and the journey, the certain and the unsure. Experiencing the drama of
the Christian Year to the full gives us space in which to live
out our faith, taking time to examine its different parts.
With its steady progress and its gradual unfolding, its different seasons and its fixed festivals, the Christian Year provides us with the perfect ritual time and space to journey
and explore, to go far and to draw near, to reside in and to
fix upon the saving power of God. A heightened appreciation of the Christian Year, therefore, can give us a deeper
and more varied spiritual life.

This closer observance of the sacred calendar can be something more than just going through the motions for ourselves. As the Apostle James pointed out, 'faith by itself, if it has no works, is dead' (James 2:17). If we want to avoid a kind of religious hypocrisy then we can ensure that a greater sense of the Christian Year also has repercussions on the way we live our lives. This is essential if our ritual life is to be meaningful rather than showy or superficial.

As individuals and as members of a Christian community, we can combine the spiritual seasons of the year with appropriate practical action. This might mean sharing our festivities with the needy, or welcoming strangers into our homes. It might mean setting specific social or pastoral objectives which present the significance of that season in concrete action within our wider community. The experience of following the cycles of the natural world through the Christian calendar also keeps us in touch with the beauty of our surroundings. It fosters a fondness and respect for God's creation and awakens us to our responsibilities to the environment, encouraging us to become more active in its protection. This is essential if we wish to avoid a time which Isaiah foresaw when 'the heavens will vanish like smoke, and the earth will wear out like a garment' (Isaiah 51:6). To this end, our Christian communities can also set themselves 'green objectives' for the different seasons of the year. These might be projects to do with environmental education, conservation or campaigning.

Finally, a heightened appreciation of the Christian Year can have a very personal effect upon us too. A closer ritual identification with the recurring mysteries of God's grace and the power of His incarnation in Christ, brings us nearer to God and to His love. And once near, His love will change us for ever. Slowly but surely, repeating the rituals of the Christian Year will, like frequent dew falls, make our faith 'blossom as the lily and strike root as the poplar' (Hosea 14:5).

THE COLOURS OF THE CHRISTIAN YEAR

For the first one thousand years of the Christian faith, the main ceremonial colour in the Western Church was white. It was not until the twelfth century that different colours began to play an important part in expressing the moods of the various seasons and holy days. These different colours were used for priestly robes, altar cloths, lecterns and other church decorations. The increasing wealth of the Church in the Middle Ages was an important factor allowing it to become more lavish in its vestments and its church design. English craftsmen became especially renowned for their ornate embroidery of clerical vestments. Their elaborate needlework was known as *Opus Anglicanum* (English Work) and was considered to be of the finest quality in the whole of Christendom.

In the early thirteenth century (1216), Pope Innocent III sanctioned the use of only four colours in the liturgy of the Western Church: white for feasts; red for martyrs; black for penitential seasons; and green at ordinary times. In the centuries that followed, a much wider use of colours has developed, so that a whole spectrum is now available in most Western churches. A notable exception are many of the

Protestant Churches, who rejected all liturgical colours
except black during the Reformation, and continue to have
a minimal use of colour today. But even in these churches,
an arrangement of fresh spring flowers and greenery with
bursting buds at Easter, or flame-red flowers at Pentecost
can enrich our understanding and our worship.

THE RAINBOW GOD

Colour is a vital and immediate ingredient in inducing festive or contemplative mood, and giving a particular orien-
tation to the soul. After the flood, God used the whole
spectrum of colours to make Himself known to human beings once again, and the rainbow is the symbol of His first
ever covenant with us (Genesis 9:8–17). We can use these
colours to emphasize different aspects of our religious
experience at different times. Colour is ever present in the
rituals of the Christian Year and is a useful spiritual prompt
as we explore the seasons of our faith. In addition to the
coloured vestments and decorations of a church, some people keep a piece of appropriately coloured cloth for each
season which they use as a book mark for a prayer book or
Bible. Wearing a piece of clothing which is the colour of
that day's season or festival is another way to bring the liturgical colours into one's daily life. These things act as a helpful reminder, or an object of meditation, at times of private
prayer, public worship, or when we are simply going about
our business. Churches now use a wide spectrum of colour
in their services throughout the year. Different colours create different moods, helping us in our exploration of that
season's meaning and significance.

Blue/Black/Purple

The dark colours of Lent and Advent have a constancy about them which draws us inwards, holding our attention. They steer us towards stillness, thought and even dreaminess, and are apt catalysts to the deeper moods of reflection, penitence and grief, which mark the seasons of Lent and certain aspects of Advent.

Red

Red holds our gaze, but challenges it too with the colour of our blood. Like the red rose, it works in us mixed feelings of beauty and pain, life and death, and pricks us with an unease appropriate to Holy Week and the commemoration of martyrs.

White/Gold

Like the sun itself, the brightness of the white and gold of major feasts cannot be looked upon for long before their light springs back at us, raising our spirits in joy. Light glitters and sparkles off these colours suffusing our surroundings with its rays. Such colours put us in the right mood for celebration.

Green

For most of the year the liturgical colour is green. The green of ordinary time is soothing and refreshing, able to nourish a broad range of emotions to match our experience of everyday life, its routine and its continuity.

Different Churches and different regions have often developed their own system of seasonal colours, but the following is a rough guide to the main colours of each season and festival. In the rest of the book, the colour for each festival and season will be given.

Festivals	White/Gold
Advent	Violet/Blue/Purple/Black
Christmas to Epiphany	White or Gold
Lent	Violet/Blue/Purple/Black
Palm Sunday to Easter Eve	Rose/Red
Easter	White/Gold
Pentecost	Red
Trinity Sunday	White/Gold
Corpus Christi	White/Gold
Apostles, Evangelists and Martyrs	Red
Saints other than martyrs	White/Yellow
Ordinary Sundays	Green
Ordinary weekdays	Green
Baptism and confirmation	White/Red
Marriage	White
Ordination	White
Funerals	Violet/Blue/Black
Dedication of a church	White

A TIME TO MOURN AND A TIME TO DANCE

By following the different moods and moments of the Christian Year, we ensure that our faith remains balanced and well rounded. By entering into the spirit of the different seasons, liturgical and natural, our own religious temper spans the whole spectrum of the Christian faith, and becomes familiar with its diversity. Carried forward by the steady current of the ritual year, we avoid getting stuck in one particular religious mood, or transfixed by a single aspect of our faith. Without the momentum of the ritual year, we might run the risk of a morbid faith which thrives on Holy Week but never moves through to resurrection. Or, we might become preoccupied with an overly enthusiastic Pentecost faith, a midsummer madness which forgets to move on again to the dark, fragile light of winter and the more profound and painful times of Lent and Holy Week, through which we discover rebirth and renewal.

Like the liturgical colours of the year, we need to weave a faith of many colours, a tapestry which glows with all the different shades of faith. Real faith is not a monotone blue-black faith, or a garish white-gold faith, but a rainbow faith which rightly reflects the diversity and perspective of the whole Christian experience.

THE ORIGINS OF THE CHRISTIAN YEAR

The calendar and liturgy of the Christian Year has developed gradually over hundreds of years. The very early Church of the first century had the most basic of all calendars. They celebrated Sundays, Easter, Ascension and Pentecost and had no other major festivals. The seasons, festivals and saints days of today's Christian Year, with their particular rituals and associations, have evolved in the 2000 years since the time of the Apostles. For example, it may seem surprising that the seasons and festivals of Christmas were not developed until the fourth century – more than 300 years after Jesus' birth.

This long and continuing growth of the Christian calendar is the sign of a healthy faith which has continually deepened its understanding of the mystery of God in Christ, and adapted itself to its surroundings in its ritual and worship. The result is a Christian calendar which provides opportunity for each of us to explore the central tenets of our faith at particular times throughout the year.

THE SANCTIFICATION OF TIME

It was not until the fourth century that the Church began to develop a more extensive calendar beyond the festivals of Easter and Pentecost, and the Christian Year took off. In 321, the Christian religion was formally recognized by the Roman state under the Emperor Constantine and Sundays were officially denoted as the day of Christian worship and a day of public rest. Until this time, Christians had been subject to persecution throughout the Roman Empire. Their various churches and communities had been forced to worship secretly at worst, and discreetly at best. But with its legalization, the Church gained a new confidence. The fourth century onwards saw Christian worship moving from the private to the public sphere, and embarking on a new period of expression and elaboration.

As the church began to take up more public space, so it also began to take up more time. Gradually, it developed an annual round of historical commemorations of the main events of Christ's life. Drawing on events recounted in the gospels and the Acts of the Apostles, the Church now made a sacred chronology of its own to fit within the seasons of the year. Dom Gregory Dix has described this process as 'the sanctification of time' (Dix, G. (1964), *The Shape of the Liturgy*, p. 303). It is this desire to create ritual time to accompany the ritual space of church buildings and services which lies at the heart of the elaboration of a sacred Christian calendar.

THE SANCTIFICATION OF NATURE

As the Church began to sanctify and Christianize time, so it also began to Christianize the events of nature and her seasons. Throughout the ancient world, people celebrated and gave thanks for the different miracles and blessings of the agricultural calendar. Particular rites and festivals were associated with spring, summer, autumn and winter in the many parts of the world which were being exposed to Christianity. Many of these ancient pre-Christian festivals were associated with fertility deities, and with the sun and the moon. As Christianity expanded and took root amongst these various communities, it overlaid its own sacred cal-endar onto the existing agricultural calendar and Christianized many of the ancient ceremonies. Priests were often involved in blessing the preparation, sowing and harvesting of the fields, and many ancient pre-Christian rites took on new Christian significance. The cross and the plough began to work the same furrow through the seasons of the year.

The agricultural calendar is dictated by the movement of the sun and the different seasons this creates. In the northern hemisphere, the sun is low in the sky during the winter months and the hours of daylight are short and cold. In the spring and summer months when the sun is high, the days are longer and warmer. The movement of the sun comes to a head in the winter and summer solstices – the two turning points in the year when the sun is respectively at its lowest and highest. The winter solstice on 21 December is the shortest day of the year. The summer solstice on 21 June is the longest day of the year. Twice each year there is also a day when the hours of daylight and the hours of night are of equal length. These days are called the equinoxes. There is a spring equinox on 21 March and an autumn equinox on 21 September. This natural agricultural calendar – with its focus on darkness and light, life and death, sowing and harvest – was taken up by Christians and made the basis for their sacred calendar.

THE TWO GREAT CYCLES: EASTER AND CHRISTMAS

The growth of the Christian Year was firmly grounded in the gospel events, and developed along the two great cycles of Easter and Christmas. As the Christian calendar expanded, festivals commemorating the gospel events were gradually unravelled along the natural cycles of the sun and the agricultural calendar. The Christmas cycle spans the autumn and winter months and includes Advent, Christmas, Epiphany and Candlemas. It has its climax on

Christmas Day around the winter solstice, the shortest and darkest day of the year. This is the season of Christ's incarnation when the new light begins to come into the world.

The Easter cycle spans the spring and summer months and includes Lent, Holy Week, Easter, Ascension Day and Pentecost. It builds up to its high points on Easter Day around the spring equinox and at Pentecost which comes before the summer solstice which is the longest and brightest day of the year. This is the season of Christ's resurrection when the light triumphs over the darkness. Feasts of the Blessed Virgin Mary are associated with the equinox. The Feast of the Annunciation on 25 March falls very close to the spring equinox and the Feast of the Nativity of Mary is on 8 September shortly before the autumn equinox.

TEMPORALE AND SANCTORALE

With the evolution of the Christian Year, two different types of festival began to be celebrated, and the calendar soon had two very different aspects to it which ran in parallel throughout the year. The first, described above, commemorated the events of the gospel and Jesus' life – like Christmas and Easter. This part of the calendar is known as the '*temporale*' (from the Latin word *tempora* meaning seasons) because it celebrates gospel events through the annual passage of time. But in addition to the *temporale*, Christians sought to remember the lives and virtues of the great Christian saints and celebrate them on an annual basis too. Particular days in the Christian Year are therefore designated as Saints' Days. A list of the major Saints' Days is given on page 194 at the back of this book. This aspect of the calendar is known as the '*sanctorale*' because it is to do with the commemoration of saints (from the Latin word *sanctus* meaning saint).

Over time, as many more saints were recognized by the Church, the *sanctorale* tended to grow at the expense of the *temporale*. The profusion of saints' days, with their particular cults and devotions, almost overshadowed the essential Christian Year in the Western Church. This was one of the major complaints of the Protestant reformers in sixteenth-century Europe who did away with much of the *sanctorale* and the veneration of saints. The focus of this book is on the *temporale* of the Christian calendar.

FEASTS OF MARY

Mary is regarded as the greatest of the saints and as such is uniquely honoured in festivals of both the *temporale* and the *sanctorale*. Since the very earliest days of Christianity, the Church has honoured Mary with a special place in its devotions because of her earthly relationship to Christ. Some of these feasts remember her specific role in the gospel stories while others celebrate her person and events from her own life.

The Marian feasts which celebrate Mary's central role in the gospel events as Christ's mother are known as vocational feasts because they refer to her particular vocation or calling as Jesus' mother. The vocational feasts include the Annunciation (25 March), Candlemas (2 February) and the Visitation (31 May). The other feasts of Mary are described as personal feasts because they celebrate her person and do not refer to specific gospel events. These personal feasts include her Immaculate Conception (8 December), her Nativity (8 September) and her Assumption into heaven (15 August). Roman Catholic and Orthodox Christians celebrate all these feasts and hold the Virgin Mary in particularly high esteem. However, Mary does not play as important a part in the liturgy and worship of some Protestant Churches who do not celebrate her personal feasts.

MOVEABLE FEASTS

The Christian calendar is not an entirely fixed calendar. Several of the most important festivals of the Christian Year fall on different dates every year. These festivals are known as 'moveable feasts'. This is because the date of Easter is different each year. Unlike Christmas, which always falls on 25 December, Easter is a moveable feast and has no fixed date. Instead, Easter Day is timed to coincide with the Sunday nearest to the Jewish feast of Passover – the time which Jesus chose for the Last Supper and his passion. Passover falls on the full moon after the spring equinox, and so Easter Day falls on the Sunday following this full moon. Every year therefore, Passover and Easter are on a different date to the year before which means that all the other festivals in the Easter sequence, like Ascension Day and Pentecost, also fall on different dates each year.

There are seven moveable feasts in the Christian calendar for which no regular annual date can be given because they change every year:

Advent Sunday	The fourth Sunday before Christmas
Ash Wednesday	The Wednesday in the seventh week before Easter Day
Holy Week	The week before Easter Day(including Palm Sunday, Maundy Thursday, Good Friday, and Easter Eve)
Ascension Day	40 days after Easter Day (a Thursday)
Pentecost	50 days or seven weeks after Easter Day (a Sunday)
Trinity Sunday	Eight weeks after Easter Day
Corpus Christi	10 days after Pentecost (a Thursday)

All the other festivals like Epiphany (6 January), Candlemas (2 February) and the Annunciation (25 March) are celebrated on the same date every year.

EMBER DAYS AND ROGATION DAYS

During the year, there are also two kinds of day dedicated to special prayer and thanksgiving. These are known as Ember Days and Rogation Days. They too have no fixed annual date and are moveable each year.

Ember Days fall in quarterly clusters of three days each throughout the year which are known as Embertides. Originally, Embertides marked key points in the agricultural calendar like sowing, harvest and vintage. In this context, the word ember has nothing to do with a flame or smouldering wood. Instead, the word is either a corruption of the Latin word *tempora* meaning seasons, or of the old English word *ymbren* which means recurring. Ember Days are the Wednesdays, Fridays and Saturdays within the weeks before the third Sunday in Advent, the second Sunday in Lent, and the Sundays nearest to the Festivals of St Peter (29 June) and St Michael of All Angels (29 September). The Friday of each Embertide is traditionally known as Golden Friday.

Originally associated with fasting, prayer and thanksgiving for crops and for those cultivating the agricultural harvest, Embertides have become a special time to pray for those involved in any form of clerical and lay ministry in the Church, or those preparing for ordination. This obviously represents a shift in focus from agricultural labour to those who labour for the longerterm spiritual harvest. As a result, Embertides are a particularly popular time for ordinations. But with their association with fertile seasons of sowing and harvest, Embertides have also always been a time to pray for pregnant mothers, or couples trying to conceive, and are considered to be an especially blessed time for children to be born. On a more administrative level, their quarterly cycle also made Embertides a preferred time for landlords to collect tithes and debts. Today, Embertides can provide a useful time to reflect on our own individual calling and on the fruits of that calling as they are made manifest in the social dimension of our faith and the actions of our lives.

Rogation Days are the Monday, Tuesday and Wednesday after the fifth Sunday after Easter, in other words, the three days before Ascension Day. The fifth Sunday after Easter is therefore sometimes known as Rogation Sunday. Rogation Days are a time of special invocation and prayer when people call upon God in earnest. Rogation comes from the Latin phrase *Te rogamus, audi nos*, which means 'we beseech you, hear us'. This phrase is a common form of response in the litanies traditionally recited at this time. A litany (from the Greek word *liteh* – meaning humble and fervent appeal) takes the form of petitions made by a priest or singers which are followed by public responses from the congregation. It usually combines petitionary prayers (for ourselves) and intercessionary or bidding prayers (for others). In these Rogation services, the litany is traditionally accompanied by a procession around the church or town – the act of circling something being a sign of protecting it.

Because of the fervent nature of the appeals made on Rogation Days, special extra days in the year can be designated as Rogation Days during times of disaster or emergency. This allows Christian communities to call upon God with special urgency in the face of particular calamities like earthquakes, floods, storms or war.

SUNDAYS AND THE CHRISTIAN WEEK

Sundays are the foundations upon which our religious calendar is built – the touchstones of the Christian Year. Sunday is at once the most important day of the week for celebration and reflection, as well as the main marker which guides us through the year and gives our most basic sense of rhythm to the passing of time. As our daily routine swings from one week to the next, Sunday is the metronome which sets the pace of our religious lives. The Christian Year is counted by Sundays more than by months and dates. People talk about the third Sunday in Lent or the fifteenth Sunday after Pentecost. In the Christian calendar, every Sunday has its own theme for worship and contemplation – a list of which is given on page 190.

Sunday is the weekly holy day for Christians because it is the day of the week on which Jesus rose from the dead (Mark 16:2, 9). The day after the Jewish sabbath, Sunday is in fact the first day of the week and was not originally a day of rest for the early Christians (Acts 20:7, 1 Corinthians 16:2). Neither was it a day of gloom and abstinence. As a celebration of the resurrection, it was like a 'weekly Easter', a day of joy when fasting and penitential kneeling were forbidden. Services took place early in the morning as the sun was coming up, to coincide with the time that Mary Magdalene and the other women followers of Jesus first discovered that he had risen.

The English word Sunday comes from the time when days of the week were named after the planets and their respective Gods. For example, Monday is named after the moon, and Saturday after Saturn. Because Sunday is the first day of the week it is named after the sun. This is also in line with the account of creation in the book of Genesis which describes God creating light on the first day of creation (Genesis 1:3–5). The English language has kept the original root of the word, while many other languages keep the phrase 'the Lord's Day', used by the early Christians. In Italy therefore the word for Sunday is Doménica.

In Christian tradition, Sunday is associated with special rites and legends. A child born on Sunday is considered to be especially blessed. He or she is said to have a special gift to see angels and to find hidden treasure. Sunday was also a time to pray around the church in procession, to sprinkle holy water on the graves of the dead, and also an appropriate time to wear new clothes or shoes to church for the first time to give thanks for these and all good things. More alarmingly for younger Christians, Sunday was also a traditional time for the 'hearing of children' who were tested on the catechism or asked to repeat the main points of the day's sermon.

WEDNESDAY AND FRIDAY

Wednesday and Friday are the other significant days of the Christian week, both traditionally set aside for fasting of some kind. Friday is still regarded as 'a day of discipline and self-denial' in the Anglican community and in many other Churches. Because the Christian week is regarded as a model of the week of Christ's suffering and death, Wednesday was a day of fasting because it commemorated the sealing of Judas' contract of betrayal. Friday was a day of fasting as it commemorated Good Friday and the day of Jesus' crucifixion. The customary eating of fish on Fridays is a relic of such Friday fasting.

THE CHRISTMAS CYCLE

Incarnation

The Christian year begins on the Fifth Sunday before Advent, which falls some time in late October or early November. During the five weeks before Advent, Christians focus on the beginning of all things and on God's revelation of Himself in the Old Testament before the birth of Christ.

The Sundays before Advent

And God saw all that He had made,
and it was very good.

Genesis 1:31

BEGINNINGS

At the very beginning of the year, we look back. We remember God's creation of the world and His creation of man and woman. We hear of the temptation and fall of Adam and Eve in the Garden of Eden and the tragic story of Cain and Abel. We then remember God's calling and promise to Abraham, His giving of the Law and the Ten Commandments to Moses and His many messages to the people of Israel through the fiery mouths of the Old Testament prophets.

TIME BEFORE CHRIST

Before Christ and the New Testament, God revealed Himself to the Jewish people in the history of Israel and in the books of the Old Testament. The weeks before Advent are an important time to meditate upon the truths of the Old Testament and the riches of its beautiful and ancient texts. It is a time to cherish the particular wisdom of the

Jewish tradition which we inherit in the Old Testament: its timeless understanding of the nature of mankind; its emphasis on God's immanence in our affairs; and its championing of justice and peace.

The Church gives thanks for the Old Testament before Advent, and welcomes it once again as an essential guide and companion on the journey of our faith. In the coming months the beauty of its verses and the truth of its revelation will shed light upon our way. They will act as scouts reporting on what lies ahead, and sound like distant echoes of what we are about to hear. As the religious texts read and studied by the earthly Jesus, they have a special place in our worship and prayer. Jesus himself said, 'I have not come to abolish the law and the prophets, but to fulfil them' (Matthew 5:17).

TIME TO HEAR GOD'S CALL

The very beginning of the Christian Year is the time to join with Abraham and hear God's call, and to accept once again the journey of faith which will take us through the coming Christian Year. Reading about Old Testament figures like Abraham, Sarah, Moses, Samuel and Elijah, we recognize ourselves, both in their moments of uncertainty and in their abiding faith. Now is the time to be found by God, as they were before us. Like these ancient people, who also were no strangers to reluctance, it is the time to say 'Here I am, Lord' (Genesis 22:1).

READINGS

Fifth Sunday   Genesis 1:1–3, 24–31a or 2:4b–9, 15–25.
Fourth Sunday   Genesis 4:1–10 or 3:1–15
Third Sunday   Genesis 12:1–9 or 22:1-18
Second Sunday   Exodus 3:7–15 or 6:2–8
Sunday Before   1 Kings 19:9–18 or Isaiah 10:20–23

A PRE-ADVENT PRAYER

Almighty God
whose chosen servant Abraham
Faithfully obeyed your call
and rejoiced in your promise
that, in him, all the families of the earth should be blessed:
give us a faith like his,
that, in us, your promises may be fulfilled,
through Jesus Christ our Lord. AMEN

From *Celebrating Common Prayer,* Society of St Francis, Mowbray, 1992

The Season of Advent

How lovely on the mountains are the feet of the herald who comes to proclaim peace and bring good news, the news of deliverance.
Isaiah 52:7

With the arrival of Advent, we start to look forward to the coming of Christ. We begin to prepare ourselves for the good news of Christ's coming and the revelation of God which will follow in the course of the year.

The word advent comes from the Latin verb *advenio* which means to come towards. It is all about an imminent arrival which is getting closer every day. The observance of Advent originated in Tours in France (then Gaul) in the fifth century. Bishop Perpetuus of Tours established a 40-day period of spiritual preparation for Christmas, which was modelled on Lent and originally began on 11 November, the Feast of St Martin of Tours. Some years later, the Pope adopted the season for the whole Church but shortened it to four weeks so as to affirm the pre-eminence of Lent as the most important season of preparation and penitence.

TIME TO TURN TOWARDS GOD

Advent is the time of John the Baptist. This strange figure is the first person to see what is coming. He is 'a voice that cries in the wilderness' (John 1:23) who tries to alert people and to turn their heads towards the one who is coming. But his mission is to prepare as well as to herald, and he seeks to turn hearts as well as heads (Luke 1:16–17). His message is simple: 'The Kingdom of God is close at hand. Repent and believe the gospel' (Mark 1:15). Advent is therefore the time to repent, which means to turn and re-orientate oneself towards God. It is a time of spiritual preparation when we make sure that we are facing the right way and ready for the good news of Christ's coming.

ANTICIPATION AND EXCITEMENT

Advent is the great season of anticipation and excitement. In the midst of winter it is a time to take up hoping once again and to keep a lookout. It is the time of joyful expectation in which we 'overflow with hope' (Romans 15:4) and celebrate the imminent coming of Christ in two different ways. First, we celebrate the expected arrival of the Christ child in his nativity or birth at Bethlehem. Secondly, we look forward to the second coming of the risen Christ in glory at the end of time.

At first glance this is cause for celebration alone. But along with a hope of Christ's second coming and his ultimate return in glory come the associated realities of death, judgment, heaven and hell. These more harrowing considerations make Advent a penitential season as well as a joyous one. In the short term we are to look with joy at the coming birth of Christ and the appearance of the Light of the World. In the longer term, we are forced to consider our own condition and to imagine the alarming possibility of permanent darkness without new light.

A MIXTURE OF EMOTION

In the Christian tradition, the anticipation associated with Advent is at once a mix of joy and dread. The season is double-edged. This mixture of emotion is symbolically represented in the image of a pregnant woman, and Advent is also the time of Mary the Mother of Jesus. Heavy with child in her last month of pregnancy, Mary's mood – that mixture of joy and dread at the prospect of giving birth for the first time – is perhaps the perfect image of the ambivalence of Advent feeling. Like Mary, we can embrace both aspects of this anticipation equally during the four weeks of Advent.

Preparation is the key to both forms of Christ's coming. In the first two weeks of Advent we can concentrate on the more penitential side of the season. We hear the message of John the Baptist and reorientate ourselves to God. At another level still, we can also develop a constant sense of spiritual alertness. This is the kind of spiritual sixth sense which Jesus urges upon us in the gospels – a readiness in which we live every moment in expectation of judgment (Matthew 25:31–46). This is the sense we need if we are to 'watch at all times, praying for the strength to stand with confidence before the Son of Man' (Luke 21:36). Finally, in the last two weeks of Advent we can concentrate on more joyful preparations as we get ready for the birth of the infant Jesus. We can begin to make merry and to decorate our homes, churches and towns, festooning them with light and colour in anticipation of Christmas itself.

A CHILDREN'S SEASON

Children are best at understanding and entering into the spirit and excitement of Advent. Jesus recognized children as a model of faith, and it is surely children who lead us at Advent and convey to us the real meaning of this season. As Advent progresses we too feel, like Elisabeth, the kick of a child within us which leaps for joy at the realization that Christ is coming (Luke 1:41).

For children, the advent calendar, the preparation of the crib, and the nativity play make this one of the most exciting seasons of the year. Each day a new window is opened on the calendar showing a picture of an advent theme, until the doors of the manger itself are opened on Christmas Eve to reveal the nativity of God's son. In the same way, a new piece is added to the manger each day in Advent building up to the placing of the infant Jesus in the crib on Christmas Eve.

Rehearsals for the nativity play with their build-up to the big day of the performance also engage children with the Christmas story. These customs obviously provide good opportunities to teach children the Christmas story slowly over Advent, and for them to discuss it, act it out and pray about it a little every day. Nativity plays have their origins in the old medieval Miracle or Mystery Plays – so-called because they were about the miracles in the Bible and the mysteries of faith. At a time when all church services and all bible readings were still in Latin, these plays on Christian themes were one of the few ways that ordinary people could learn about the gospel stories.

Children the world over enter into the spirit and excitement of Advent. In Latin America, the nine days before Christmas, known as the novena, are an occasion for children to rush through the streets throwing firecrackers and expressing their delight at the approach of Christmas. In Central Europe the novena are known as the 'golden nights' when children carry statues of Mary and Joseph to a new house each night and then finally to the church on Holy Night. This custom recalls the Holy Family's search for somewhere to stay. There is also a custom which runs from St Thomas' Day (21 December) until Christmas Eve in Eastern Europe, where children run around at night cracking whips, ringing handbells and wearing masks to drive away demons. These nights are called the 'rough nights' and symbolize the fact that the powers of evil are soon to be put to flight by the birth of Christ.

A SEASON OF NEW LIGHT

Many other traditions are associated with Advent in the Western Church. Among them are the advent star, the advent wreath and advent lights. The advent star was developed by the Moravian Church in Germany in the middle of the eighteenth century. Originally made of paper, but now often made of tinsel, it is hung alone or on the top of Christmas trees. It has a threefold symbolism: it signifies the star which rose in the East to guide the three Wise Men (see Epiphany); it testifies to the greatness of God as creator of the stars (Genesis 1:16), and it also identifies the coming Christ as the 'bright morning star' (Revelation 22:16).

The advent wreath is also German. It was introduced by the Lutheran community in Germany, but has its origins in the ancient festivals of light which traditionally took place at this time of year around the winter solstice. As the sun reached its lowest ebb, these ancient light rituals, with their bonfires and torches, would seek to encourage the sun by keeping lights burning in the darkest days. The advent wreath is set with five candles, four round the outside and one within it. Each of the outer candles represents one of the four gifts of the Holy Spirit: hope, joy, peace and love. Starting with a single candle on Advent Sunday, a candle is lit each Sunday in Advent until all four are burning on the Sunday before Christmas – the darkest time of the year. The candle in the middle is known as the Christ candle and is not lit until Christmas Day. This light ritual symbolizes the keeping of the faith even in the darkest moments, and is closely akin to the use of candles at Chanukah, the Jewish festival of light, which also takes place over the eight darkest days in December. The more modern public version of advent lights is the array of festive street lights which adorn our cities throughout Advent and Christmas.

In keeping with the theme of this season, all these Advent customs are cumulative, building up to a crescendo. Their nature is gradual and preparatory, and the emotions they inspire mix patience and thought with anticipation and excitement. At all times throughout the expectation of Advent, there is no doubt that Christ and Christmas will come.

READINGS

Advent 1   Luke 21:25–33 or Matthew 25:31–46
Advent 2   John 5:36b–47 or Luke 4:14–21
Advent 3   John 1:19–28 or Matthew 11:2–15
Advent 4   Luke 1:26–38a or Matthew 1:18–23

ADVENT PRAYERS

At Advent we should try the key to our heart's door. It may have gathered rust. If so, this is the time to oil it, so that it may open more easily when the Lord Jesus wants to enter in at Christmas time! Lord, oil the hinges of our heart's doors that they may swing gently and easily to welcome your coming.

Prayer of a New Guinea Christian,
The Lion Prayer Collection, ed. Mary Batchelor, Lion Books, 1992

Let not our souls be busy inns that have no room for Thee and Thine, but quiet homes of prayer and praise where Thou mayest find fit company; where the needful cares of life are wisely ordered and put away; and

wide sweet spaces kept for Thee, where holy thoughts
pass up and down, and fervent longings watch and wait
Thy coming.

Prayer from the Lucknow Diocese, North India
in *Morning, Noon and Night: Prayers and meditations mainly from the Third
World*, John Carden, CMS, 1976

The Season of Christmas

The light shines in the darkness, and the
darkness has not overcome it.

John 1:5

Christmas is a time of great joy. It celebrates the birth of Christ and the wonderful mystery of the incarnation, in which the eternal Son of God was made man and 'dwelt among us' (John 1:14). The season of Christmas lasts for 12 days between Christmas Day on 25 December and the Feast of Epiphany on 6 January.

The English word 'Christmas' refers to the day's celebration of the Mass of Christ. Most other languages, like the Italian *Natale*, refer to Christ's birth. The French word *Noel* however, comes from the old word 'nowel' which means news, and refers to Christmas as the time of good news. German names for Christmas refer to Holy Night, while the old English word Yule recalls the Anglo-Saxon winter solstice festival of *geola*.

ORIGINS

The feast and season of Christmas was introduced in Rome in the early part of the fourth century, probably around AD 330. It is perhaps the best example of the early Church Christianizing the traditional non-Christian festivals of a season – in this case the festivals of returning light surrounding the winter solstice. Christmas successfully took on many of the trappings of these more ancient festivals – several of which are still with us today.

In ancient Rome it was the custom to celebrate the Feast of the Sun God on 25 December. This winter solstice celebration was known as the 'Birthday of the Sun' and was a time of great joy and feasting. It was also common in the classical world to celebrate the birthday of history's great men on an annual basis.

The newly recognized Christian community in Rome at this time decided to combine these two customs in a new Christian festival which celebrated the nativity of Christ at the time of the winter solstice. Chronologically, it matched Luke's account of Jesus' conception in 'the sixth (Jewish) month' (Luke 1:26) which is equivalent to our third month, March, some nine months before Christmas. Theologically, it provided the perfect calendar setting for the celebration of Christ as the 'light of the world' (John 8:12) and as 'the sun of righteousness [which] shall rise with its healing wings' (Malachi 4:2).

Christmas has since become the most widely celebrated of all Christian festivals. The sense of irrepressible joy at the news that 'God is with us' combines with a natural need to celebrate in the midst of winter and with an equally universal feeling of gladness which surrounds the birth of a child. But Christmas has not always been cherished by all Christian communities – particularly in the wake of the Reformation in Europe in the seventeenth century. In England the celebration of Christmas was outlawed by the Puritans in 1642 and its festivities were banned by Parliament in 1647 along with 'all other superstitious festivals'. Many of the British people rioted as a result. Christmas celebrations were broken up by force in the years that followed until in 1660 Christmas was restored, along with the monarchy. In New England in North America, Christmas remained banned until the second half of the nineteenth century. 25 December was a common working day in Boston right up until 1856.

SON AND SUN

The close association of Christmas with the winter solstice and its 'pagan' rituals has always alarmed some parts of the Christian community. But the connection need not be a source of anxiety. Knowing that God is Lord of the sun, moon and stars, an appreciation of the world's natural cycles serves to enhance our understanding of His revelation in Christ. Just as Jesus used the ways of nature to expound religious truth, so we too can look upon nature's recurrent patterns as parables which complement our understanding of Christ's life, death and resurrection.

Christmas Eve

*In the morning you shall see the glory
of the Lord.*
Exodus 16:7

Christmas Eve officially belongs to the Season of Advent.
But because the ancient service of Midnight Mass gets underway before midnight on Christmas Eve, in practice it is
treated as part of the Christmas Season.

A NIGHT OF VIGIL

Christmas Eve, or Holy Night, is one of the two great vigils
of the Christian Year – the other being at Easter. If Advent
has been a time to prepare for and watch out for the coming of Christ, then Christmas Eve is the night of the final
vigil before the dawn which brings his birth. The word vigil
comes from the Latin word for wakefulness and watching,
and the ancient service of Midnight Mass is usually the best
attended service of the whole Christian Year.

A SACRED NIGHT

Many old Christian legends are associated with Christmas
Eve. It is said to be a night when the power of evil is suspended, and when ghosts and witches are rendered power-
less. It is a night of miracles when nature too rejoices and
worships the infant Christ. In particular, many things are
linked with the stroke of midnight which tradition gives as
the exact time of Christ's birth.

Legend has it that cattle fall to their knees in stables
while deer kneel in homage in the forests. Bees awake temporarily from their winter sleep and hum beautiful tunes
which only those dear to God can hear. Sparrows are said to
sing like nightingales and every bird sings through the
night in praise and celebration. Animals are granted the
gift of speech on Holy Night and talk like humans to spread
the word of Jesus' birth. Trees and plants bow down in rev-
erence towards Bethlehem, and the peal of bells rings out
from the bottom of wells whose water has special powers of
healing on this sacred night. At the well in Bethlehem itself, the original Star of Bethlehem is seen to glide across
the surface of the water in the depths of the well – the water
having never given up its original reflection of this most
holy star. For people too it is a special time. A Catholic legend has it that the gates of heaven are opened briefly at
midnight so that any person who dies at that time can go
straight there, reprieved from any time in Purgatory.

CHRISTINGLE SERVICES

Christmas Eve (or sometimes the Sunday before Christmas) is also the time for the increasingly popular Christingle services. These are special services for children which involve a symbolic celebration of the Christmas mystery by giving every child a 'Christingle' which is made of an orange, a candle, ribbons, nuts, raisins, sweets and cocktail sticks! The top of the orange is hollowed out to hold the candle, around the base of which is tied a white ribbon. Four cocktail sticks are then stuck into the skin of the orange, on the end of which are nuts, raisins and sweets. A red ribbon is then tied round the middle of the orange.

The word Christingle probably comes from the German *Christ-engel* (Christ angel) or *Christ-kindl* (Christ child). It has its origins in the Moravian Church which first developed the custom of giving children Christmas candles tied with a red ribbon at a Christmas Eve service in 1747 at Marienborn in Germany. In Britain in the nineteenth century, the symbolism of the candle was developed with the addition of the orange and its sweets. The symbolism of the Christingle is readily understood by children. The orange is the world; the white ribbon represents purity; the cocktail sticks are the four seasons; the nuts, raisins and sweets are God's gifts to his children; the lighted candle stands for Christ as the light of the world; and the red ribbon surrounding the orange is the sign of His blood with which He redeems the world. Holding the Christingle in front of them, children have an immediate and appealing symbol which speaks at once of creation, incarnation and redemption.

THE CHRISTMAS CRIB

Christmas Eve is also the time to move the completed crib into the church for the duration of the Christmas season. The first crib was made by St Francis of Assisi on Christmas Eve at Greccio in Italy in 1223. With his love of animals he created a nativity scene with real animals so that people could come and contemplate the circumstances of Christ's birth, and recognize the special place of animals in God's purpose. His idea took off and the creation of a model crib has since become an important way of re-enacting and exploring the main themes of the nativity. St Francis also started the custom of being especially kind to animals at Christmas, giving them extra feed or special shelter, as a reminder for their presence at Christ's birth.

READING

Luke 1:67–79

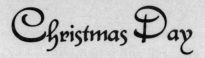

Christmas Day

WHITE OR GOLD

The grace of God has dawned upon
the world with healing for all mankind.

Titus 2:11

With dawn on Christmas Day, the waiting is over, our expectations are fulfilled, and our joy is complete. From the darkest of dark nights, the light of God's purpose amongst us is rekindled in the birth of a child.

GOD WITH US

The joy of Christmas is the joy of the incarnation. The good news of Christmas and the incarnation is that God is not far off, but has come near to us; has identified with us; experienced our lives, and shared our world. On Christmas Day we realize that God is here.

The joy and peace of Christmas affects us all. It is almost tangible in the air itself on Christmas Day and we cannot help but spread it. In the gospel stories, the shepherds cannot contain their emotions and are bursting with the news. They tell everyone they meet and people are amazed at what they hear (Luke 2:17–18). The sheer infectiousness of Christmas with its message of peace and joy is captured in an ancient Christmas ritual of the Syrian

Church. After the eucharist at Midnight Mass, the priest leans over the altar rail and touches the person nearest to him, who in turn touches his neighbour. The 'touch of peace' is then spread throughout the whole congregation in something similar to a Mexican wave.

THE UNEXPECTED

But at Christmas we also recognize that the good news is not that simple. With the birth of Christ we are still only at the beginning of the year and at the outset of God's plan of salvation. We have the good news but do not understand it all, and are yet to see the consequences for ourselves. Like Mary, in the midst of all this celebration and joy, we hear the good tidings but also 'ponder them in [our] heart' wondering what it will all mean (Luke 2:19). For if Christ's birth is a reason for joy, it is also an occasion for reflection and even bemusement. Because, strangely, after all the waiting and expectation of Advent has come the unexpected.

The kindling of God's light is not some glorious and triumphal fireball which takes the world by storm. Instead, it is the merest flicker, a newborn baby, the weakest and most vulnerable form of human being. Here begins the mystery and paradox of the incarnation: the life of Christ which reveals that God's ways are often contrary to expectation. The infant Jesus is the smallest of lights, yet that light will brighten a way that will challenge us more than we could have believed possible, and reward us more than we could possibly have hoped.

In Christ's nativity, the Christmas story introduces the essential unexpectedness of God's revelation. Christmas brings the realization that all through the longing of Advent we could really not have known what we were to expect because this is a new thing that God does. The baby Jesus and the cold cradling from which his life begins, reveal that God's ways are not the ways of men. He comes not in strength but in weakness, and His wisdom seems like folly. God turns our world on its head and has a virgin for a mother, a baby for a King, and a manger for a cot.

This Christmas theme is at the very heart of the Christian faith which comes to see that 'the foolishness of God is wiser than men and the weakness of God is stronger than men' (1 Corinthians 1:25). On the Feast of Christ's birth this particular truth of Christianity is revealed, a truth which will be made clear throughout the rest of the year.

CHRISTMAS TREES, GREENERY AND MISTLETOE

Many customs are associated with the season of Christmas. Although many of these are now begun earlier in Advent, like the Christmas tree, yule log, mistletoe, holly, carols, Christmas cards and Christmas presents, they really belong to the Christmas season proper.

The Christmas tree has its origins in medieval times when mystery plays were performed in Advent, and Christmas Eve (24 December) was commemorated as the Feast Day of Adam and Eve. Many of the mystery plays retold the story of Adam and Eve and had a 'paradise tree' as a prop on stage. This tree was usually a fir tree decorated with apples, reminiscent of the tree in the Garden of Eden. Over time it became popular to put such a tree inside the home on 24 December as well, to commemorate the first parents and to remember the earth's greenery in the midst of winter. In sixteenth-century Germany, the custom of the paradise tree became combined with that of traditional Christmas lights to produce the modern Christmas tree. The apples on the tree, with their reminder of our sin, were offset by the lights and their symbolism of our redemption. And today, the round baubles on many Christmas trees continue to represent the fruit on the original paradise tree. German immigrants first took the custom of the Christmas tree to America in the eighteenth century. Queen Victoria's husband, Prince Albert, introduced the Christmas tree to Britain and set up the country's first Christmas tree at Windsor Castle in 1841.

The yule log was an especially big log which was cut to provide fuel for cooking and heating for the whole of the Christmas season. Its selection, cutting and lighting were an exciting time, and every year the new yule log was kindled with the remains of last year's log which had been kept all year for the purpose. In Europe, the ashes from the yule log were also kept to be spread as particularly holy fertilizer on the fields at Plough Monday (the first Monday after Epiphany) when the ploughing season traditionally began.

Mistletoe has a special place in Christmas custom, particularly in Britain where it was the most sacred of all plants to the ancient Druids. In old English, mistletoe means 'all healing' because the plant was renowned for its powers of healing and fertility. Mistletoe grows high in the trees, and was so sacred that even enemies who met underneath it in the forest would lay down their arms, greet each other and keep a truce for a day. At Christmas today, sprigs of mistletoe are hung in doorways as a token of peace and goodwill to all comers. And the ancient custom remains that if you pass beneath it with someone you must embrace and kiss. From its pre-Christian roots, the tradition about the healing properties of mistletoe has become a powerful Christian symbol of the peace between ourselves and our fellows, and between ourselves and God, which Christ brings at Christmas time.

Other evergreen plants have also become closely associated with Christmas decoration. Although many of these are still used today, paper decorations have become more common. But all this is a sign that the pre-Christian traditions of decoration at this time of year have been absorbed into the Christian celebrations and are alive and well. Holly, with its strong green leaves and bright red berries, is a natural form of decoration in the dark months of Christmas. It has also attained a certain Christian symbolism. Its thorns tell of the crown of thorns which the infant Jesus is destined to wear around his head, with the red berries being like the beads of his blood. The ivy, so closely associated with holly, was the ancient symbol of the wine god Bacchus and his revels. The laurel wreath is the ancient symbol of triumph and symbolizes God's victory in Christ the King.

In recent years, poinsettia has emerged as a favourite plant of the Christmas season. This bright red plant comes from Central America where it blooms at Christmas time and is known as the 'flower of Holy Night' – its red pointed leaves said to resemble the star of Bethlehem. It takes its more mundane name of poinsettia from the American Ambassador to Mexico, Dr Poinsett, who introduced it to the USA in 1851. The herb, rosemary, is also associated with the Christmas season, because of a legend that Mary dried the baby Jesus' clothes on a rosemary bush during their flight into Egypt.

CAROLS, CARDS AND MYSTERIOUS PRESENTS

Christmas carols are an old form of entertainment which have their origins in medieval ring dances accompanied by singing. These were extremely popular in Italy, Spain, France, Germany and England, where many such songs were written specially to celebrate the Christmas season. Christmas cards took off when cheap postage became available in the second half of the nineteenth century. The first Christmas cards were printed in London in 1842.

The tradition of associating Christmas with the giving and receiving of presents is an old and varied one, with many cultures having their own particular myth of the secret gift-bringer who gives presents to children at night. In some countries it is Christ, in others it is a mythical old man or woman. In Russia an old lady brings presents to children. This act is said to be her eternal penance for misdirecting the Magi when they sought the birthplace of Christ, or for turning away the Holy Family when they were searching for somewhere to stay the night. She now makes up for this by giving presents to all children at the feast of Christ's birth. In other parts of the world, Santa Claus, or Father Christmas, is the secret present-giver. This merry figure who lives deep in the cold polar areas has emerged from a combination of St Nicholas, the patron saint of children, and Thor, the great Nordic God of the north. St Nicholas traditionally gave children presents on his feast day on 5 December. But with the Protestant abolition of many saints' days during the Reformation, this custom was transferred to Christmas Eve. In Italy the Fairy Queen gives gifts at Epiphany rather than Christmas.

MINCE PIES AND CHRISTMAS PUDDING

Christmas pudding and mince pies are the high point of every Christmas feast. In traditional mince pies, the mincemeat was put into little crib-shaped pastries to recall Christ's nativity. Both the mincemeat of the pies and the mixture of the pudding were made long before Christmas Day. Anglicans made them on 'stir up Sunday'. This is the last Sunday before Advent when the collect for the day starts with the words 'Stir up, we beseech thee, O Lord, the wills of thy faithful people'. This was the day to start mixing and stirring the mince pies and Christmas puddings.

READINGS

Luke 2:1–20
John 1:1–14

CHRISTMAS PRAYERS

Almighty God,
you have shed upon us
the new light of your incarnate Word,
giving us gladness in our sorrow
and a presence in our isolation:
fill our lives with your light
until they overflow with gladness and praise,
through Jesus Christ our Saviour. AMEN

From *Celebrating Common Prayer*

May the humility of the shepherds
the perseverance of the wise men
the joy of the angels
the peace of the Christ Child
be God's gift to you (us) this Christmastide and always.

Mervyn Stockwood in *Short Prayers for the Long Day*, ed. Giles and
Melville Harcourt, Collins, 1978

Holy Innocents 28 December

RED

See that you do not despise one of these little ones; for I tell you that in heaven their angels always behold the face of my Father who is in heaven.

Matthew 18:10

The Feast of the Holy Innocents commemorates the massacre of all male children under two years old in and around Bethlehem by order of King Herod (Matthew 2:16). The massacre was an attempt to kill the infant Christ whom the wise men had described to Herod as the King of the Jews. Jesus escaped after a warning in a dream to Joseph, and the Holy Family fled to Egypt (Matthew 2:13–15). The feast falls on 28 December and is also known as Childermas Day. Because the feast remembers a massacre of the innocent, the liturgical colours change temporarily from the white and gold of Christmas to the red of martyrdom.

THE SPECIAL STATUS OF CHILDREN

The Feast of Holy Innocents is occasion to reflect upon the particular place of children in the world. Advent and Christmas Day are the season and festival which children relish above all others. During these festivities we have ample time to see for ourselves the enthusiasm and spontaneity of children, and their enormous capacity for enjoyment. The Feast of Holy Innocents and the horrors of infanticide which it remembers is brutal testimony to the fact that children are also extremely vulnerable. While they seldom play any part in shaping the decisions and events of the adult world, they are frequently the first to suffer their effects. In wars, famine, floods and political oppression children often suffer first and frequently suffer more than adults.

The protection and birth of the Christ Child from Herod's massacre is an opportunity to remember the rights of all children. Holy Innocents is a moment in the midst of the celebration of childhood at Christmas to look at the adult world's responsibilities to children. The fact that God took the form of a child shows the special place of children in creation. Jesus himself affirmed this special status when he said: 'See that you do not despise one of these little ones; for I tell you that in heaven their angels always behold the face of my Father who is in heaven . . . So it is not the will of my Father who is in heaven that one of these little ones should perish' (Matthew 18:10, 14). The massacre of the innocents is a resounding reminder of how often adult society can ignore and abuse the special status of children.

A MODEL OF FAITH

Jesus also recognized the particular gift of religious under-standing which children possess and their special place in the Kingdom of Heaven (Mark 10:13–16, Matthew 18:1–4). He made clear that 'whoever does not receive the kingdom of God like a child shall not enter it' (Mark 10:15). Jesus' teaching emphasized that Christian faith requires the openness, trust and immediacy of a child. As usual in the Kingdom of God, which has just been heralded by the birth of an impoverished child, the normal way of the world is turned on its head. In keeping with the unexpectedness of Christmas, Christ's teaching reveals that in the Kingdom of Heaven it is adults who need to learn from children.

READING

Matthew 1:13–18

Epiphany (6 January)

WHITE OR GOLD

I am the light of the world; he who follows me will not walk in darkness, but will have the light of life.

John 8:12

The Feast of Epiphany remembers the adoration of the Magi, or wise men, who followed a new star from their distant lands in the East to the stable in Bethlehem. They travelled many miles convinced that the star would lead them to a newborn king. When they arrived they worshipped the baby Jesus and presented him with gifts of gold, frankincense and myrrh. Christian tradition has always regarded their gifts as profoundly symbolic and prophetic. The gold recognizes Christ's heavenly kingship. Frankincense is a fragrant resin which is burned as incense to symbolize the presence of God and so recognizes Christ's divinity. And myrrh is a precious oil used for anointing the body, which serves to foretell Christ's death.

Epiphany marks the end of the Christmas season and falls on 6 January. Epiphany Eve (5 January) is known as Twelfth Night as it comes twelve days after Christmas. The season of Epiphany – the third season of the Christian year – runs for six weeks after 6 January.

THE THREE WISE MEN

Many legends have grown up around the Magi which provide personal details about them beyond the Biblical description of their visit. Because they gave three gifts, it has long been assumed that there were three of them. Because of their riches, it has also been thought that they were kings so that the three wise men are also portrayed as three kings. Because these three wise kings are seen to represent all the nations of the world, tradition has also made one white, one black and one Asian.

Legend has even given names to the three kings who are known as Melchior, Caspar and Balthazar. They are often represented as travelling in three ships, as in the carol 'I Saw Three Ships Go Sailing By'. This legend refers to their journey home. Having arrived by camel or on horseback, it assumes that they must have returned by sea after they were warned in their dream not to travel via Jerusalem where they might have disclosed the secret of Christ's birthplace to King Herod (Matthew 2:12).

Many customs surrounding Epiphany draw on the story of the Wise Men. Traditionally, in Italy, Spain and Latin America, it is at Epiphany rather than Christmas that presents are mysteriously given to children. In Spain, the Magi leave little presents in children's shoes. In many cultures children dress up as the Wise Men at Epiphany and parade through the streets. The three Wise Men and their star also play a major part in children's nativity plays at Christmas, and the paper crowns worn at Christmas remember these three kings as well as Christ's own kingship at this time.

On a more administrative level, the Feast of Epiphany was also the time in the ancient Eastern Church when the Christian scholars and astronomers of Alexandria would announce their calculations of the timings of the coming Christian calendar to the whole Church and set the dates of Easter and the other moveable feasts.

TAKING DOWN THE DECORATIONS

Twelfth Night, the night before the Feast of Epiphany, marks the end of the Christmas celebrations. As Epiphany approaches it is customary to replace the shepherds in the crib with images of the three Wise Men. Finally, when the Feast of Epiphany is over it is the traditional time to take down the Christmas decorations and put them safely away for another year.

PLOUGH MONDAY

Epiphany was also the time to put away the remains of the yule log, storing it in a dry place to kindle next year's log. The Monday after Epiphany was known as Plough Monday when all the ashes from the yule log over the past twelve days were collected up and sprinkled on the fields to bless them and make the earth fertile once again as ploughing began again. At the same time, the priest would also bless the ploughs, a custom which still continues today in some farming communities.

WATER RITUALS

Epiphany also recalls the baptism of Christ and is therefore a traditional time for water rituals. Holy water is blessed for the font at Epiphany. Rivers and lakes were also traditionally blessed at this season and mass dunkings took place in the Jordan and the Nile. Homes were also blessed for the New Year at Epiphany. In some countries, they were sprinkled with holy water and the date of the new year would be chalked on the inside of the door alongside the initials of the three wise men: C, M and B.

The Season of Epiphany

GREEN

I will make you a light to the nations, to
be my salvation to the earth's farthest bounds.
Isaiah 49:6

The Greek word *epipheneia* means manifestation or show-ing, and was used to describe the official state visit of a king or emperor to a city or region of his kingdom – a rare occasion when he publicly showed himself to his people, usually in dazzling splendour. The season of Epiphany recalls the first public appearances of the adult Christ and his announcement of the Kingdom of Heaven to Jews and Gentiles alike. It is the time in the gospels when his nature and purpose suddenly shine forth in glory and he begins to work his wonders upon the earth in his public ministry.

A LIGHT FOR THE WHOLE WORLD

If Christmas has seen the light of God rekindled in the world, then Epiphany shows that light coming into view, being seen by others and casting its brightness upon all people. It records the mystery of the incarnation as it moves beyond the private sphere of the Holy Family and the crib to the public sphere of the world beyond. At the heart of Epiphany is the conviction that in Jesus, God shows

Himself not just to the Jewish community, but to all the peoples of the world. Such universalism is enshrined in the Epiphany story of the Wise Men from the East.

After the last of the nativity stories about the coming of the Magi, the readings for this season move forward rapidly to the beginning of Jesus' adult life. The first Sunday in Epiphany celebrates the baptism of Christ and the beginning of his ministry. The following weeks remember the calling of his disciples, his first miracle at the wedding at Cana, his first confrontations with the religious authorities, and his early teaching in parables.

The six weeks of Epiphany are about appearance, visibility, recognition and public action. Having come into the world at Christmas in the form of a newborn baby, God now sets out to challenge and heal the world through the ministry of the adult Christ. After the glimmerings of Advent and Christmas, the light of the world now shines clearly in the world and will become ever brighter as Jesus' earthly ministry takes its course through the rest of the Christian Year.

CONFLICTING CROWNS AND KINGDOMS

Kings and crowns are a major theme of Epiphany. There are the wise kings who come from the East, the wicked King Herod in Jerusalem and the extraordinary new king born in poverty in Bethlehem. During the season of Epiphany, this new king proclaims the Kingdom of Heaven and the reign of God on earth. But this strange and puzzling kingdom stands at odds with the power and kingship of the world, and will eventually lead to the new king being mocked in royal robes and bleeding from a crown of thorns.

Introducing the image of kingship, the Epiphany story lays a trail of questions about authority, obedience and justice which recur repeatedly throughout the Gospel. How just is the power which is robed in splendour and dwells in palaces? To whom do we owe obedience? At Epiphany, as the light of the world becomes manifest in Christ, it is visible to good and bad alike, to the Wise Men and to Herod. Both react very differently to it. Now in the open for all to see, Christ's life on earth and the pattern of the Christian Year which follows it, are set to bring both joy and confrontation.

READINGS

Epiphany 1   Matthew 3:13–17 or John 1:29–34
Epiphany 2   Mark 1:14–20 or John 1:35–51
Epiphany 3   John 2:1–11 or 6:1–14
Epiphany 4   John 2:13–22 or 4:1–14
Epiphany 5   Matthew 12:38–42
Epiphany 6   Matthew 13:24–30

AN EPIPHANY PRAYER

We have read, O Lord, about the Wise Men of the East who were guided to you by a star and who brought generous gifts of gold, frankincense and myrrh; give us the wisdom to seek you, light to guide us to you, courage to search until we find you, graciousness to worship you and generosity to lay great gifts before you, who are our King and our God for ever and ever. AMEN

From *Words for Worship*, ed. C. R. Campling, Edward Arnold, 1977

Candlemas (2 February)

Suddenly the Lord whom you seek will come to his temple;
the messenger of the covenant in whom you delight is here.

Malachi 3:1

The Feast of Candlemas falls on 2 February and marks the Purification of the Virgin Mary and the infant Christ's Presentation at the Temple. These two ceremonies take place forty days after the birth of a child according to Jewish law and Candlemas is therefore often known by both these other names as well.

The story of the baby Jesus' Presentation in the Temple, and in particular, his meeting with two prophets, Simeon and Anna, is recorded in Luke's gospel (Luke 2:22–35). These elderly people both recognize Jesus instantly as the 'light to lighten the nations' and feel able to die in peace, content that God's purpose is once more being acted out.

BRIGHT CANDLES AND HOLY WAX

The Feast of Candlemas is above all a festival of light. In northern climates, it comes as a timely and much needed reminder of light when we have just struggled through the seemingly endless grey days of January. Candlemas acts as something of a spiritual reviver to pep us up and keep us moving on our way from winter to spring, Christmas to Easter. It can be valued and enjoyed as something of a tonic.

Celebrations of Candlemas are begun on Candlemas Eve with a candlelit procession which enters the darkened church as a sign that Christ has brought light to the world. The next day, on the Feast itself, all church candles are then consecrated for use during the coming year. Candles themselves have an important significance for Christians. The candle is a sign of divine light but is also an important symbol of Christ's incarnate nature. All church candles must be made of beeswax, as bees were believed to have escaped from Paradise and were also famous for their virginity. The virgin wax of the candle thus represents Christ's sinless human flesh which burns with the divine fire that makes him also God. In the evening of Candlemas Day, some people light a special candle and drink mulled wine or punch, with the children being allowed to stay up for as long as the candle burns.

A FESTIVAL OF MARY

Candlemas is an important Marian Festival too and remembers Mary's purification after the birth of Christ. Under Jewish law, a woman stays at home to recover and nurse her child for forty days after the birth of a child. At the end of the 40 days she then presents herself at the temple (or today the synagogue) to give thanks for her child and for her safe delivery, and to purify herself before taking up her public position in society once again.

PREPARING FOR SPRING

Christianity recognized the need for a festival of light and cleansing to break up the monotony of the winter months and to remind people that spring would reappear. Pagan festivals in Europe traditionally celebrated light and newness at this time of year and Christian Candlemas draws on these ancient rituals.

In medieval Europe, early February was a time to get ready for the next agricultural season. It is also the time when the ewes come into milk in preparation for lambing.

On 1 February, now Candlemas Eve, people processed round the fields, waving torches and 'beating the bounds' with sticks. This reaffirmed farmers' boundaries and was believed to banish evil winter spirits, purify the fields and invigorate the soil in readiness for sowing. Not to be outdone, townspeople also marched around the city walls, reaffirmed the powers of light over their town and started the spring cleaning. Candlemas, then, is the time to put winter behind us and set our sights on the spring ahead.

WEATHER FORECASTS

Candlemas is not just the time to prepare for the coming spring weather but also the day to predict it. The weather on Candlemas Day is said to indicate the coming weather for the next few weeks. If the weather is fair on Candlemas Day, then winter is not yet over. But if the weather is bad, then the rhyme has it that 'winter is gone and will not come again'. In some parts of the world, people take their meteo-rological cues from animals on Candlemas Day. Germans study the behaviour of badgers to see if winter is past. In the USA, 2 February is called Groundhog Day, when ground-hogs are supposed to emerge from hibernation. If the sun is shining and the groundhogs can see their own shadow, then winter will last another six weeks. If it is cloudy, they know that winter will soon be over. For a day at least, such animal surveillance might make a welcome change from satellite forecasts and computer predictions.

More importantly than weather forecasts, the Feast of Candlemas allows us to continue to affirm God's light in the world, picking up where Christmas and Epiphany left off, and anticipating Easter and spring. The Feast of Candlemas provides an important bridge between the two Christian cycles of Christmas and Easter. Still in the early part of the year, it remembers Jesus the child. A festival of light, cleansing and renewal, it begins the true turning of the year.

READING

Luke 2:22–35

A CANDLEMAS PRAYER

O thou great Chief,
light a candle in my heart,
that I may see what is therein,
and sweep the rubbish from thy dwelling place.

African School Girl's Prayer, *The Oxford Book of Prayer*,
ed. George Appleton, Oxford University Press, 1985

THE EASTER CYCLE

Resurrection

After the season of Epiphany the Christian Year moves
once more towards a period of preparation, this time
for the greatest of all Christian feasts – Easter. From the
Ninth Sunday before Easter until Easter Day itself, the
Christian Church gradually engages in its most intense
period of penitence and prayer. The sacred calendar
slowly plumbs its greatest depths in Lent and Holy Week,
before suddenly soaring to the moment of its greatest
joy on Easter Day.

Pre-Lent and Shrovetide

GREEN

Grant to your faithful people pardon and peace:
that we may be cleansed from all our sins
and serve you with a quiet mind.
(*ASB*, Collect for Sunday before Lent)

The three Sundays before Lent are traditionally known as Septuagesima, Sexagesima and Quinquagesima because they are approximately seventy, sixty and fifty days before Easter. From the fifth century onwards, these three Sundays before Lent (now known as the ninth, eighth and seventh Sundays before Easter) became a preparatory period of confession, absolution and feasting in readiness for the rigours of Lent. The idea of a seventy-day period before Easter was seen to coincide appropriately with the seventy years the Israelites spent in captivity and exile in Babylon.

The last three days before Lent (Sunday, Monday and Tuesday) are known as Shrovetide. This old English word comes from the verb 'to shrive' which means to 'write down'. It dates from the days when people would confess their sins and then receive absolution and a written list of their Lenten penance from the priest. This pre-Lenten practice was known as being shriven.

The readings for this period continue to recall Christ's public ministry of teaching, healing and forgiveness. In church services the joyful words of Alleluia and the Gloria are sung or said for the last time before Easter. Both priest and people refrain from uttering them again during the sad days of Lent until they can be resoundingly reaffirmed at the triumph of the resurrection early on Easter morning.

CONFESSION AND FORGIVENESS

The pre-Lenten period is the time to look back at the last year, to confess and receive absolution for our sins. It is also the time to plan our penitential regime and to decide what we will give up during Lent. We can also decide what we will take up for Lent. For Lent is not simply about denial but also about social action and alms-giving. In the three weeks before Lent, plans can be made individually or as a church about which particular projects to carry out over the forty days of Lent.

Shrovetide is a time to be forgiven and to forgive. Jesus' teaching about forgiveness in the gospel reading for the Sunday before Lent is clear (John 8:2–11). To those who would condemn he says: 'Let him who is without sin among you throw the first stone'. And to those who have sinned: 'Neither do I condemn you; go and do not sin again.' Recognizing our own sins and showing forgiveness to others is the spirit of these pre-Lenten days.

CARNIVALS

But the days before fasting are also the last chance for feasting. When penance and fasting were engaged upon in earnest in Christian communities, a pre-fasting period of celebration and revels was always enjoyed before the deprivations set in. These feasts would get underway in the three weeks before Lent alongside the penitential preparations of confession and absolution. This was the time to eat in abundance the foods which were about to be forbidden. It was also the time for revels like dancing, races and ball games.

One of the main restrictions of the traditional Christian fast was on the eating of meat. Quinquagesima or Shrove Sunday (the last Sunday before Lent) was the time to abstain from eating meat, and so meat feasts and games abounded at this time. This was known as carnival time, from the Latin phrase *carnem levare* which means to 're-move meat'. It referred to the fact that there would be no meat on the table for the next forty days.

SHROVE TUESDAY

These pre-fasting festivities soon came to be concentrated on Shrove Tuesday, the day before the beginning of Lent, when all feasting foods were eaten for the last time before the long fast. Pancakes are the main food of Shrove Tuesday celebrations in many carnivals because they are fried in the butter or animal fat which was forbidden in Lent and because they can be filled with all the delicious delicacies which will be prohibited in the weeks ahead. Tossing pancakes is still one of the games associated with Shrove Tuesday and stems from the old pre-Christian springtime rituals of this time of year which celebrated the return of the summer sun. With its circular golden brown shape, the pancake was seen to represent the sun. By tossing it higher and higher people encouraged the sun to rise higher again in the sky and signal an end to the short, dark days of winter.

In France, the Tuesday before Lent is known as Mardi Gras (Fat Tuesday) because of its pre-fast feasting. In many other parts of the world today, the days before Lent are still carnival time. Some of the most famous carnivals of all are held in New Orleans, Rio de Janeiro and Venice.

READINGS

9th Sunday before Easter   Matthew 5:1–12 or Luke 8:4b–15
8th Sunday before Easter   Mark 2:1–12 or 7:24–37
7th Sunday before Easter   Mark 2:13–17 or John 8:2–11

SHROVETIDE PRAYERS

God in heaven, you have helped me to grow like a tree.
Now something has happened. Satan, like a bird, has
carried in one twig of his own choosing after another.
Before I knew it he had built a dwelling place and was
living in it. Tonight, my father, I am throwing out both
the bird and the nest.

Prayer of a Nigerian Christian, *The Oxford Book of Prayer*

Almighty God,
Unto whom all hearts be open,
all desires known,
and from whom no secrets are hid:
cleanse the thoughts of our hearts
by the inspiration of thy Holy Spirit
that we may perfectly love thee,
and worthily magnify thy holy Name;
through Christ our Lord,
AMEN

Alternative Service Book, Church of England,
SPCK/Clowes/Cambridge University Press, 1980

The Season of Lent

If you would live, resort to the Lord.

Amos 5:6

Lent is the most important period of penitence and prayer in the Christian calendar. It is a time of fasting, self-examination, reflection and meditation. It is also a time of alms-giving. As far back as 461, Pope Leo I instructed that 'what we forgo by fasting is to be given as alms to the poor'.

Lent lasts for forty days in memory of the forty days in which Christ was tempted in the wilderness (Luke 4:2). In many languages, the name for this period of penance refers to these forty days, like, for example, the Italian word *Quaresima*. But in English the word Lent comes from the old English word for Spring, 'Lengten'. It refers to the lengthening days of early spring when the sun rises higher in the sky and shines longer on the earth.

LENTEN VEILING

The solemnity of Lent is reflected in the liturgy and church services of the season. In addition to the omission of the Alleluia and the Gloria, church organs traditionally remain silent and no weddings are celebrated during Lent. Flowers are no longer displayed in the church, except on Sundays, and the so-called Lenten array is put up around some churches. Plain or purple cloths are used to cover crosses, crucifixes, pictures and statues in the church. This custom is known as Lenten veiling and the coverings often have simple designs on them which hint at the object which lies hidden behind them. In the Middle Ages, it was the custom to draw a large curtain in front of the altar itself to conceal it from view. This curtain was kept drawn throughout Lent, except during the Eucharist on Sundays, until it was finally and dramatically pulled aside in Holy Week at the moment in the Passion Narrative which describes the tearing of the temple curtain at Jesus' death (Luke 23:45).

CATECHUMENS, QUARANTINE AND SCRUTINIES

Lent has its origins in the fourth century where it was introduced as a period to prepare people for baptism at Easter. The so-called 'catechumens' endured a harsh period of induction at a time when the Church was sceptical about the real conviction of those becoming Christians in the new Holy Roman Empire. For forty days, would-be converts were put through a rigorous programme of prayer and penance and refrained from washing, eating rich food and sexual relations. Throughout Lent they were also subjected to regular 'scrutinies' or interrogations on the Creed and principles of the Christian faith in front of the congregation. Finally, if all went well, they were baptized at the Easter vigil.

In the centuries which followed, the ordeal of the early catechumens formed the basis for Lent becoming a more universal period of penance for everyone. While most people carried out their fast and penance alongside their normal way of life, some people were singled out to make public penance for particular antisocial offences they may have committed the previous year. These people were not allowed into church during Lent and were set apart from their family and community. Made to go barefoot and wear sackcloth, they were sent to a solitary place to live in isolation for the forty days of Lent. They were not allowed to talk to anyone and were forbidden to shave, cut their hair or have a bath. In Latin this form of penance was known as 'quarantine' (from *quaranta* meaning forty) from which the modern concept of medical quarantine is derived. Many devout people chose to adopt some similar form of penitential regime for themselves, and Lenten retreats are still a common form of Lenten preparation for Easter, but these are not so harsh nowadays!

DO NOT LOOK GLOOMY

Jesus stressed that fasting and penance should not be a showy and extravagant affair. The spirit of Lent looks inwards rather than outwards. It is a time of private self-examination which takes its inspiration from Jesus' lonely struggle to resist temptation in the wilderness. The forty days of Lent give us the time and space to recall and confess past sins. They also allow us to strengthen ourselves by thinking about our attitudes and behaviour so that we can change and resist temptation in the year ahead.

TAKING SOMETHING UP FOR LENT

But Lent is not all introspection. It is also a time to be active in the world and to use such activity as the basis of meditation and prayer. Lenten activities make clear the age-old Christian conviction that Lent is as much about taking something up as it is about giving something up.

Many people choose a special religious book to read during Lent to concentrate the mind on spiritual matters. Lent books are often recommended by bishops or chosen by parishes. A book can be read individually or by a group of people who meet regularly during Lent to discuss it, meditate upon it and pray together. But Lenten study need not be confined to books. A series of paintings, cassettes, plays and films can also be the subject of discussion and meditation. Some people might choose to go on a course of some kind. Others might make a commitment to visit particular places during Lent and then discuss and meditate upon their experience there. Such places might include unknown corners of the parish, hospitals, prisons or local beauty spots.

Lent is frequently being used these days as an opportunity for ecumenical or inter-faith encounters. To this end, people from one parish might set up a series of exchanges with churches from different denominations or with people from neighbouring Moslem, Hindu, Jewish or Buddhist communities – many of whom also have particular religious festivals around this time of year. At a personal level, Lent may also be a good time to commit oneself to a series of meetings with people one has fallen on bad terms with in the year just past in an effort to make one's peace again.

THE TWO PHASES OF LENT

Lent divides into two main parts – penance and
Passiontide. In the first four weeks we think about ourselves
and concentrate on penance and personal transformation.
In the last two weeks we contemplate the Way of the Cross.
The fifth Sunday in Lent is known as Passion Sunday and
begins the period known as Passiontide. This two-week period includes Holy Week and concentrates on the suffering
of Jesus' last days. It is a time to consider the implications
for our lives if we take up Jesus' challenge and follow him
in the Way of the Cross.

READINGS

Lent 1   Matthew 4:1–11 or Luke 4:1–13
Lent 2   Luke 19:41–8 or Matthew 12:22–32
Lent 3   Luke 9:18–27 or Matthew 16:13–28
Lent 4   Luke 9:28–36 or Matthew 17:1–13
Lent 5   John 12:20–32 or Mark 10:32–4

A PRAYER FOR LENT

O Lord Jesus Christ, you taught your disciples to pray, to do good deeds and to fast cheerfully, without hypocrisy or ostentation; help us to use this season of Lent sincerely for your service, so that we may pray more, do more and discipline ourselves cheerfully for your sake; for you died for us but now you live, for ever and ever, world without end. AMEN

From *Words for Worship*

Ash Wednesday

You are dust and to dust you shall return.
Genesis 3:19

Ash Wednesday is the first day of Lent. It is named after the church rituals of that day in which the priest makes the sign of the cross in ashes on the foreheads of the faithful. Traditionally known as the 'imposition of the ashes' (but more commonly known as 'ashing'), this ritual dates back to the sixth century and is a powerful way to start Lent. Ash Wednesday is also sometimes known as Pulver Wednesday from the Latin word *pulver*, meaning powder or dust. The first Sunday in Lent after Ash Wednesday is traditionally known as Quadragesima – being some forty days before Easter.

For thousands of years, ashes have acted as a symbol of purification and penance in many of the world's religions. Purified by fire, the soft ashes of some previously living thing remind us of the frailty of our life. The ashes used in the Ash Wednesday service are the ashes from the burnt palm crosses of the previous Palm Sunday which are mixed with holy water. The priest dips his thumb into the mixture and makes the sign of the cross on people's foreheads. The grey cross on the forehead serves to remind people of the sins they have committed and is a public sign of their repentance and contrition.

READINGS

Matthew 6:16–21 or Luke 18:9–14

Mothering Sunday

VIOLET/PURPLE

As truly as God is our Father,
so truly is God our Mother
Julian of Norwich

The fourth Sunday in Lent is called Mothering Sunday because it was the day when people were encouraged to return to worship in their 'mother church' where they had been baptized. For those people who still regularly worshipped in their home church, Mothering Sunday was an occasion to visit and worship in the cathedral instead, the mother church of their diocese.

Mothering Sunday is the one day of joy in Lent, when flowers abound in church once more and people feel some relief from the rigours of the penitential season. It is also known as Mid-Lent Sunday, Refreshment Sunday or Laetare Sunday. The Latin name of Laetare Sunday refers to the word *Laetare*, meaning rejoice, which is the first word of the Introit for this day in the old Roman Missal.

A DAY ABOUT MOTHERHOOD

In the Middle Ages, Mothering Sunday became a particular holiday for all young people working as apprentices away from home. They would visit their villages and often take presents to their mothers, so giving Mothering Sunday a double purpose as a religious and a family day. Mothering Sunday was also a traditional time to propose marriage, probably because it gave young people the chance to return home and visit an old childhood sweetheart or provided an occasion to take their new love home to meet the family.

Today, children still honour their mothers on Mothering Sunday. In many British church services, children go up to the altar where they are given daffodils by the priest. They then take their daffodils and present them to their mothers and grandmothers as a token of their love and gratitude.

Mothering Sunday is also a good opportunity to broaden our understanding of God by reflecting upon God as our mother as well as our father. In the fourteenth century, Julian of Norwich (the first woman to write in modern English) experienced and understood the motherhood of God in her visions. Mothering Sunday is a good time to share her vision and to recognize that although we are distinguished by our gender, God is not. Instead, God is both mother and father to us.

MOTHER'S DAY

Mothering Sunday is not to be confused with the more modern innovation of Mother's Day which comes from the USA. Mother's Day was started by Anna Jarvis in Philadelphia in 1907 to remember the contribution of mothers after her own mother had died on 9 May of that year. Mother's Day was later made official by the US government in 1914 as a day to honour and remember all mothers. Mother's Day falls on the second Sunday in May when people give presents to their mothers and treat them with a day of rest and enjoyment. In some parts of the world people wear a carnation on Mother's Day – a red one to remember a mother who has died or a white one as a sign of thanks to a mother who is still alive.

SUNDAY OF THE ROSE

In the Roman Church, the fourth Sunday in Lent is also known as the Sunday of the Rose from an ancient custom in which the Pope always returned from Mass on this day carrying a golden rose. The vestige of some ancient Spring-time flower ritual, this practice became Christianized because the rose is the symbol of the Virgin Mary and was also seen to refer to Christ as 'the flower sprung from the root of Jesse'. Each year the Pope would send the golden rose to a Christian prince or king who had been especially loyal to the Papacy or championed the Faith in some way during the previous year. King Henry VIII of England received the golden rose from the Pope on two occasions. Needless to say, this was before the Pope refused to grant him a divorce from Catherine of Aragon and Henry separated the Church of England from the Church of Rome.

READINGS

Luke 9:28–36 or Matthew 17:1–13

A PRAYER FOR MOTHERING SUNDAY

God our mother,
you hold our life within you;
nourish us at your breast,
and teach us to walk alone.
Help us to receive your tenderness
and respond to your challenge
that others may draw life from us,
in your name, AMEN

From *All Desires Known*, Janet Morley, SPCK, 1992

The Annunciation

Hail Mary, full of grace, the Lord is with you.
Luke 1:28

Around the time of Mothering Sunday, the calendar continues to dwell on motherhood by remembering the mothering of Christ himself on the Feast of the Annunciation. This feast falls on 25 March which is usually sometime during Lent and is also known as Lady Day in England in honour of the Virgin Mary.

MOTHER OF GOD

The Feast of the Annunciation celebrates the Angel Gabriel's appearance to the Virgin Mary when he announces to her that she will conceive and bear a son to be called Jesus. This story, known as the annunciation, is told in the gospel of Luke (1:26–38) and has inspired some of the greatest paintings and poems in Christian art throughout the centuries. Gabriel's words of greeting to Mary have become the first part of the famous 'Hail Mary' prayer which is said widely throughout the Roman Catholic Church. The feast was originally known as the 'Conception of Christ' and still is in the Orthodox Church. It marks the start of the incarnation, the very instant when the word of God begins to be made flesh.

The Feast of the Annunciation celebrates Mary's unique role in our salvation, as well as the more general significance of women as intermediaries between God and the world. At the annunciation, it is a woman who is first made aware of God's purpose in Christ and who bears the incarnate Christ as the mother of God. Similarly, on Easter Day it will also be a woman, Mary Magdalene, who is first made aware of the resurrection and bears news of the risen Christ to the other disciples. The role of the Virgin Mary as the mother of God shows how female experience is in many ways the first to light upon a sense of the divine. In Mary, God shows clearly how He chooses women as the mothers of His purpose and how they hold a central place in the Kingdom of Heaven. This is an essential message for the Christian Church whose worship has for centuries been dominated, and to some extent distorted, by men.

WOMB AND TOMB

Falling as it often does in Lent, the Feast of the Annunciation comes as a strange moment of intense hope and excitement during so sad and serious a season. Just as we are looking towards the moment of Christ's death and his burial in a tomb, so we also find ourselves remembering his conception in the Virgin's womb. Mary's pregnancy reminds us of the very miracle of life and creation and its ability to recreate itself time and again. It reminds us of how God renews His presence amongst us day after day, year after year. He is never absent, ever near.

Even as our minds are looking towards the sorrow and tragedy of the Passion, we hear Gabriel's announcement once again. As we meditate upon the end of Christ's earthly life in Lent, we already know that his incarnation will be renewed amongst us. For as things are coming to an end, so they are also starting again. The overlap between Annunciation and Lent makes all this plain. The way of God is a ceaseless round. We may celebrate the story of His love consecutively throughout the seasons of the Christian Year, but in reality He moves amongst us simultaneously, working out His purpose as a whole and not in part.

SEEDTIME

The Annunciation is a relatively early feast and was first celebrated in the East in the fifth century, arriving in the West at Rome in the sixth and seventh centuries. 25 March was obviously chosen as the feast day because it is exactly nine months before Christ's birth at Christmas Day on 25 December, the natural period of human pregnancy.

In the northern hemisphere, the timing of the Feast of the Annunciation means that it takes place shortly after the spring equinox on 21 March, when day and night last for exactly the same time. This is the traditional time for sowing and planting the seed of the summer crops. Indeed, sowing traditionally got underway the day after the Feast, in accordance with the old rhyme that when 'St Gabriel to Mary flies, this is the end of snow and ice'. At this time in the agricultural calendar therefore, people's thoughts are on sowing and new life, just as they are in the Annunciation's celebration of fertility and the conception of Jesus.

In Rome, the Popes used the Feast of the Annunciation as an occasion to positively encourage the sacrament of marriage and human fertility. On the day of the Feast, the Pope would give 300 poor maidens 50 gold pieces each to provide them with the means to make an honourable and appropriate marriage. In church services, medieval liturgy often dramatized the gospel's account of the encounter between Gabriel and Mary. The gospel would be read or sung as a dialogue between the two, with a narrator taking the voice of Luke the evangelist. In a more elaborate and risky medieval German version, a choirboy would be lowered from the ceiling singing the part of the Angel Gabriel. As he hung suspended, the excited children in the congregation would stare upwards in amazement. Their mothers would then put packets of sweets behind them on their pews as if the real Angel Gabriel had flown past and done so while the children were distracted.

MEDIEVAL NEW YEAR

In medieval times, before the introduction of the new calendar in 1752, the spring equinox marked the beginning of the new year. And 25 March – the Feast of the Annunciation – was New Year's Day. It was a time of great excitement, but also a day of legal and financial obligations. As the end of the final quarter of the year, 25 March was the last day on which all rents and debts were collected. Even today, although the calendar year now runs from January to December, the legal and financial year still runs from April to April. The end of March is still a busy time for companies, accountants and lawyers, many of whom close their books on 31 March and produce their annual reports.

THE FEAST OF SWALLOWS

In Europe, the Feast of the Annunciation is also known as the Feast of Swallows, because it is around this time that the swallows return from their African migration and take up their old nests in Europe once again. As the old Austrian rhyme has it: 'When Gabriel does the message bring, Return the swallows, comes the spring'. In many parts of central and northern Europe, swallows are therefore known as 'Mary's birds' or 'God's birds'. They are considered especially sacred and one should never kill a swallow or destroy their nests. The first Christian Crusaders to the Holy Land discovered that the city of Nazareth itself, where Gabriel appeared to Mary, is a favourite place of swallows. It remains so to this day, confirming that this beautiful, gregarious bird with its fast and exhilarating flight has a special link to the Virgin Mary and the Angel Gabriel.

THE VISITATION

Soon after the annunciation in Luke's gospel, the Virgin Mary journeys to visit her friend Elisabeth, who is pregnant with John the Baptist (Luke 1:39–56). It is at this meeting that Elisabeth's baby 'leaped for joy' in her womb when he heard the pregnant Mary greet his mother. Elisabeth instantly recognizes that Mary is carrying the saviour of the world and utters what has come to make up the second part of the Hail Mary prayer: 'Blessed are you among women and blessed is the fruit of your womb'. Mary responds with her famous words which begin 'My soul doth magnify the Lord and my spirit rejoices in God my saviour'. In these verses she praises God as a God of justice who keeps His word and who has bestowed great favour on her. Mary's words are known by the Latin word *Magnificat* (magnifies) from its first line, and have always been a central part of Christian liturgy.

This meeting between Mary and Elisabeth, and their two babies who recognize one another from the womb, is known as the Visitation of the Blessed Virgin Mary to Elisabeth. It is celebrated as a separate Feast of Mary on 31 May. Like the annunciation, it also plays an important part in the Advent readings leading up to Christmas.

READING

Luke 1:26–38

ANNUNCIATION PRAYERS

Hail Mary, full of grace,
the Lord is with thee.
Blessed art thou among women,
and blessed is the fruit of thy womb, Jesus.
Holy Mary, Mother of God,
pray for us sinners, now, and at the hour of our death.
AMEN

We beseech thee, O Lord, pour thy grace into our hearts; that as we have known the incarnation of thy Son Jesus Christ by the message of an angel, so by his cross and passion we may be brought into the glory of his resurrection; through the same Jesus Christ our Lord.

Feast of the Annunciation, Western Rite, in *The Oxford Book of Prayer*

Passiontide

VIOLET/PURPLE

'We are now going up to Jerusalem,' he said, 'and the Son of Man will be given up to the chief priests and the doctors of the law, they will condemn him to death and hand him over to the foreign power.

Mark 10:33

The fifth Sunday in Lent is traditionally known as Passion Sunday and marks the beginning of Passiontide which recalls Jesus' final journey to Jerusalem, his suffering and death. The word Passion comes from the Greek word *pasko* meaning to suffer and has come to refer to the last days of Jesus' earthly life when he is betrayed, tried, humiliated and crucified. These final two weeks of Lent are especially solemn. In them, we make the transition from reflecting upon ourselves to remembering Christ's suffering and death.

THE WAY OF THE CROSS

On Passion Sunday we turn with Christ towards Jerusalem and begin to make the Easter journey with him – meditating upon the way of the Cross and the hard truth of his teaching:

> if any man would come after me, let him deny himself
> and take up his cross and follow me. For whoever

would save his life will lose it, and whoever loses his life
for my sake will find it (Matthew 16:24–5).

During the first week of Passiontide we have time to meditate upon the paradox of this spiritual truth. In the second
week of Passiontide, known as Holy Week, we will re-enact
this truth by remembering the particular historical events
of Christ's Passion.

READINGS

John 12:20–32 or Mark 10:32–45

A PASSIONTIDE PRAYER

Christ give us grace to grow in holiness,
to deny ourselves,
take up our cross
and follow you.

Adapted from the *Alternative Service Book*

Holy Week

RED

Unless a grain of wheat falls on the ground and dies,
it remains a single grain: but, if it dies,
it yields a rich harvest.

John 12:24

Holy Week is the most sacred time of the whole Christian Year. It is known as the Great Week in which we remember, day by day, hour by hour, the last moments of Christ's earthly life and their mysterious events which form the basis of our faith.

ORIGINS

The rituals and services of Holy Week took the form we now know in fourth-century Jerusalem when Christians were no longer persecuted and were free, for the first time, to worship openly. While generations of Christians had celebrated Easter for over three hundred years since the first Easter, they were now able to do so openly in the actual places where the Easter mystery had originally unfolded.

The church in Jerusalem, and the many pilgrims who flocked to it at this time, devised a ritual week which recalled and acted out the events of Jesus' suffering, death and resurrection. The special services and ceremonies of

Palm Sunday, Maundy Thursday, Good Friday and the Easter Vigil took shape and the week soon became a ritual replica of the last days of Christ's life. The new rituals immediately struck a chord with the wider Christian world, and Holy Week as we know it rapidly became the cornerstone of the Church's annual worship.

RE-LIVING THE PASSION

Holy Week recalls the story of Christ's suffering and death, known as the Passion Narrative. During the week, we remember and meditate upon the events of each day of that original week long ago as if they were happening again today. On Palm Sunday we enact Jesus' entry into Jerusalem surrounded by an applauding crowd. On Monday and Tuesday we remember Jesus and his disciples' preparation for the Jewish feast of Passover. On Wednesday we recall the day when Judas made a deal with the authorities to betray Jesus and hand him over to them. On Maundy Thursday, we remember the Last Supper when Jesus commanded his disciples to love one another and gave them the Eucharist as a way of remembering him. The early morning of Good Friday was the time of Jesus' agony in the Garden of Gethsemane, when his three disciples slept beside him, unable to keep watch and pray with him. On that same day Jesus is arrested, put on trial and crucified. On Holy Saturday we share the grief of Jesus' family and disciples and mourn with them.

EASTER GARDEN

A tradition of Holy Week is to make a miniature Easter Garden and place it in the church. This is a small model of the garden and tomb where Jesus was buried, but can also include a replica of his cross. Like the crib at Christmas, the Easter Garden is a good way to bring the events of Holy Week to life for children and allow them to be actively involved in the celebrations and services.

A HOLY WEEK PRAYER

Father in heaven, as your people prepare once more
to follow the events of Good Friday and Easter,
may we be led by your Spirit to deeper insights
into your love and saving grace;
that we may love you more and serve you better,
for the sake of him who died for us and rose again,
our Lord and Saviour Jesus Christ.

Roger Pickering in *Contemporary Parish Prayers*, ed. Frank
Colquhoun, Hodder & Stoughton, 1975

Palm Sunday

RED

Blessed is he who comes in the name of the Lord!
Hosanna in the highest!
Matthew 21:9

Holy Week begins with Palm Sunday, which is the Sunday before Easter and the sixth Sunday in Lent. As this is the first day of Holy Week, the liturgical colours change from the purple of Lent to the red of martyrdom.

TRIUMPHAL PROCESSION

Palm Sunday is named after the palms which people carried when Jesus entered Jerusalem for the last time. He came with his disciples and was greeted by a great crowd, many of whom 'took branches of palm trees and went out to meet him' (John 12:13) and 'carpeted the road with their cloaks, and cut branches from the trees to spread in his path' (Matthew 21:8). In the ancient world, the palm was a symbol of triumph waved before conquering heroes and kings returning from victory in battle.

In Jerusalem, this event is still re-enacted every year in a procession into Jerusalem from the Mount of Olives. The same procession is imitated in and around churches throughout the world on Palm Sunday. The congregation sing hymns and carry crosses made out of palms, pussy willow or blossom (depending on the region) and church doors are often used to symbolize the gates of Jerusalem. People traditionally keep their palm crosses as a sacred memento throughout the year, often as bookmarks in their Bibles, or as pendants in their houses or cars. In Italy there is a custom of giving your palm cross to someone you are on bad terms with as a sign of reconciliation.

READING THE PASSION NARRATIVE

Palm Sunday is a day of rejoicing and a day of great sadness. We start by raising our voices and crying Hosanna with the crowd, welcoming Jesus in triumph to Jerusalem, but this is also the day when the whole Passion Narrative from the gospel is read for the first time in church at a single sitting. Listening to the Passion Narrative, the day's initial feelings of triumph and recognition are gradually overshadowed by contemplation of Christ's suffering which is to follow.

The Passion Narrative is often read or sung from alternating sides of the church. Different voices take different parts in the story and are led by a narrator. This practice dates back to the fourth century and has evoked some of the most powerful sacred music in the Christian tradition. Originally the narrative would have been chanted by priests in a plainsong. Christ's voice was always sung as a bass with the narrator as a tenor and the words of the crowd screeched out in the high-pitched voice of an alto. By the eighteenth century, passion music had become extremely elaborate. It had changed from Gregorian chant for three voices into full-blown oratorios for orchestra and choir. Bach's *St Matthew Passion* and *St John Passion* are probably the most famous examples of these oratorios.

READING

Mark 14:32–15:41

A PALM SUNDAY PRAYER

Jesus, King of the Universe;
ride on in humble majesty,
ride on through conflict and debate,
ride on through sweaty prayer and betrayal of friends,
ride on through mockery and unjust condemnation,
ride on through cruel suffering and ignoble death,
ride on to the empty tomb and your rising in triumph,
ride on to raise up your Church, a new body for your service,
ride on, King Jesus, to renew the whole earth in your image;
in compassion come to help us. AMEN

Prayer from Andhra Theological College, Hyderabad
in *Morning, Noon and Night*

Monday, Tuesday and Wednesday in Holy Week

RED

There are no special services on the next three days of Holy Week. They represent the three days that Jesus and his disciples spent preparing for the Passover Feast in Jerusalem – the annual feast when Jews remember their delivery from slavery in Egypt. The gospel readings for these days continue to read from the Passion Narrative. Having started with the version from St Mark on Palm Sunday, the other gospel accounts of Jesus' Passion are now read in turn over the different days of Holy Week.

THE PASSION STORY

Listening to the various accounts of Jesus' last days reminds us of how many people are involved in the story. Some had very significant parts to play, like Judas and Pontius Pilate. Others were more on the fringe of events, like Simon of Cyrene, the two thieves and even Peter towards the end. Although the Passion Narrative is very short by the standards of today's storytelling, it has a very large cast. These next three days of Holy Week are a good time to think about the members of that cast and the different roles they played around Jesus as he held centre stage.

We hear about the woman who devotedly pours expensive oil over Jesus' head and anoints him. She understands that Jesus is going to die before even the disciples have really grasped the fact. Judas then negotiates with the religious authorities and seals a contract to betray Jesus for thirty pieces of silver. At the Last Supper, their last evening together with Jesus, the disciples are still unwilling to accept what is about to happen and are confused about the consequences for themselves. After the Last Supper, Jesus retreats to pray in the Garden of Gethsemane with Peter, James and John who keep falling asleep while Jesus is racked with agony about what awaits him in the morning and prays to be spared it.

As the morning of Good Friday dawns, Judas and the authorities arrive in the garden. Judas then betrays Jesus with a kiss, and some of the disciples try to take up swords to protect Jesus. At his trial before the religious authorities, we hear the vehemence of those accusing Jesus. His trial before the Roman authorities is remarkable for Pilate's vacillation and reluctance, and for the dream of Pilate's wife who warns him not to shed innocent blood by executing Jesus. Then in response to Pilate's indecision and his offer of a pardon, a determined and bloodthirsty crowd chooses the release of a criminal, Barabbas, instead of the release of Jesus. Sentenced to death, Jesus is then assaulted and mocked by his Roman guards who dress him up in the purple robes of a king and a crown of thorns. In the meantime, as Jesus prophesied, Peter denies any knowledge of Jesus three times before the cock crows.

As Jesus is led stumbling to his crucifixion under the weight of his own cross, Simon of Cyrene steps in to help him and a crowd of women watch weeping as he passes by. At a hill called Golgotha, he is finally crucified in between two thieves. One of the thieves taunts Jesus and derides him as a fraud. The other recognizes Jesus' innocence and asks him for his blessing. Finally, with his mother and the women disciples looking on, Jesus dies. At the moment of his death, the curtain into the most holy part of the Temple in Jerusalem is torn in two and darkness descends upon the earth. A Roman centurion who witnesses Jesus' death is suddenly convinced of his innocence and holiness. Then Joseph of Arimathea, who was a senior member of the Jewish religious authorities and spoke out against Jesus' sentence, secures permission from Pilate to take Jesus' body. He wraps it in a shroud and buries it in a rock tomb.

This is the story of Jesus' last days as we hear it, albeit told slightly differently, in one gospel account after the other.

SPY WEDNESDAY

In Ireland, the Wednesday in Holy Week is traditionally known as Spy Wednesday. This is the day of the week when we particularly remember Judas' part in Jesus' death. Although the word 'spy' is never used of Judas in the gospels, he certainly plays the part of a traitor: the insider who changes sides and betrays his own friends. While still pretending to be a loyal disciple, Judas is in fact in league with the Jewish authorities and has made a secret pact with them. Being privy to information about Jesus' movements, he passes this information to the authorities so they can arrest Jesus more easily, agreeing to identify Jesus by kissing him.

The reading from Matthew on the Wednesday in Holy Week recalls Judas' bitter regret when he learns that Jesus has been condemned to death. It tells how, disgusted with what he has done, he returns the thirty pieces of silver and then commits suicide by hanging himself.

READINGS

Monday	Matthew 26:1–30 or Luke 22:1–38
Tuesday	Matthew 26:31–75 or Luke 22:39–71
Wednesday	Matthew 27:1–56 or Luke 23:1–49

Maundy Thursday

RED (WHITE AT HOLY COMMUNION)

*Jesus said: 'A new commandment I give to you,
that you love one another, as I have loved you.'*
John 13:34

Maundy Thursday, or Holy Thursday, is the day of the Last
Supper. It remembers when Christ washed the feet of his
disciples, gave them his new commandment to love one
another, and led them in the Holy Eucharist. The word
Maundy comes from the Latin phrase *mandatum novum*
meaning 'new commandment'.

Coming immediately before Good Friday and the three
great days of Easter, Maundy Thursday is full of anticipation and has come to be crammed with liturgical significance over the centuries. Several different rites were, and
still are, traditionally carried out on Maundy Thursday, cul-
minating in the evening Eucharist which remembers the
washing of the disciples' feet and the first Eucharist in the
upper room the night before Jesus died.

RECONCILIATION OF PENITENTS

In the early church, Maundy Thursday was the time for a
service of reconciliation for the public penitents, who after
so many days of fasting and isolation were in a fairly

wretched state. Lying face down in the doorway of the church as the Litany and Miserere were sung at the morning Eucharist, they would eventually be led up to the bishop or priest and receive forgiveness for their sins. With their penance complete at last, they would then leave the church and have their first bath and shave since the beginning of Lent in preparation for the three most holy days of Easter and their readmission to the Eucharist at Easter. Indeed, Maundy Thursday was a time for everyone to wash and prepare clean clothes for Eastertide and so was often called Clean Thursday.

FEET WASHING AND MAUNDY MONEY

The idea of cleansing was also linked to Jesus' washing of his disciples' feet at the Last Supper. Traditionally, this gesture of love and humility has been re-enacted by bishops and priests through the centuries who wash the feet of twelve people on Maundy Thursday. In England, the medieval kings and queens used to wash the feet of as many people as they were years old. But today, the Queen gives specially minted Maundy money instead to the same number of people as the years of her age. In even-numbered years the Maundy money ceremony is celebrated in Westminster Abbey and in odd-numbered years it takes place at different places around the British countryside. As well as their Maundy money, Elizabeth I used to give specially chosen subjects an elaborate wicker hamper, known as a maund, full of food and cloth.

BLESSING OF THE OILS

Just as Candlemas is the occasion in the Christian Year to bless the church candles for the year, Maundy Thursday is the day to bless the holy oil. The new holy oil is then used during the year ahead for baptism, confirmation, ordination and for anointing the sick and the dying.

THE BIRTHDAY OF THE EUCHARIST

Maundy Thursday has often been known as the 'birthday of the Eucharist' or the 'birthday of the chalice' because it remembers Jesus' institution of the very first Eucharist at the Last Supper. After their supper together, Jesus instructed his disciples to take bread and wine in remembrance of him, to be his body and his blood. From this moment on, the Eucharist became the central and most holy part of Christian liturgy and worship. The most momentous part of Maundy Thursday is the evening communion service, or mass, which celebrates Jesus' giving of the Eucharist. At this service, the red vestments of Holy Week are temporarily put to one side and the white vestments of a feast day are worn in celebration of Christ's great gift to his Church.

In the Roman Church, it has long been the custom to reserve, or put aside, a portion of the sacrament from this mass in a very sacred place for special veneration. This particularly elaborate Holy Week container or repository was known in Latin countries as a *monumento* and was often displayed somewhere very high up in the church. In the medieval church, people would try to visit and pray before seven *monumenti* on the night of Maundy Thursday.

SHARING A SPECIAL SUPPER

Jesus placed great importance on sharing meals with people and the gospels often recall him eating with friends. Jesus' last meal with his disciples before he died – the Last Supper – was the special supper for the annual Jewish feast of Passover. Known as a 'Seder', this meal is still celebrated by Jews today and involves readings, songs and the eating of special food like lamb and bitter herbs which symbolize the story of the Jews' suffering and captivity in Egypt.

In the first five hundred years of the Church's history, Christians continued to value meals and met regularly to share a meal on Sunday evenings. These suppers were often called 'agape meals', from the Greek word *agape* meaning love. When the Church was still illegal and meeting in secret, it seems likely that these meals would have been the time at which people shared the Eucharist.

An increasing number of Christian communities today are reviving some form of communal meal on Maundy Thursday (or another day earlier in Holy Week) to remember the Last Supper and the institution of the Eucharist. Whole congregations will often organize large events where they eat together, usually grouped in tables of twelve to represent the twelve apostles who were with Jesus at the Last Supper. The various courses of the supper are mixed with worship, readings and prayer. Holy Communion is often celebrated during the supper in memory of the very first Eucharist. Similar agape meals can also be organized at home on Maundy Thursday for friends and family. Agape meals in Holy Week or on Maundy Thursday are largely solemn occasions, happening as they do on the eve of the saddest day of the Christian Year. They are a powerful way to remember the last days of Jesus' life and to be together as a family or congregation in the midst of Holy Week.

There is a growing trend to make Holy Week agape meals into exact replicas of the kind of Passover meal which Jesus himself might have celebrated at the Last Supper and which Jews still celebrate today. In so doing, some Christians seek to 'Christianize' this Jewish feast by incorporating Christian readings and Holy Communion within the texture of a distinctly Jewish ritual. This custom has proved to be insensitive and caused serious offence to some parts of the Jewish community. Because of this, it is better to keep any agape meal as a uniquely Christian meal. If members of any church want to understand the festival of Passover it is better to ask a local Rabbi to lead a congregation through a demonstration Seder or to go as a guest to a Jewish Seder.

THE HOLY GRAIL

The chalice used by Jesus in the Eucharist at the Last Supper has become famous in legend as the 'Holy Grail' – from an old French word, *greal*, meaning platter or dish. The story goes that Joseph of Arimathea used this cup to collect some drops of Jesus' blood at the crucifixion. He then brought the chalice, or grail, secretly to England and hid it somewhere near Glastonbury. The quest for the Holy Grail became the great preoccupation of King Arthur's Knights of the Round Table, with Perceval, Bors and Galahad finally succeeding in the quest when they find the grail and take it to Arthur's court. Here it was guarded by the Knights until Sir Galahad's death when it was miraculously carried up to heaven.

THE STRIPPING OF THE ALTAR

At the end of the evening Eucharist on Maundy Thursday, the altar is stripped of its coverings and washed. Any other church furnishings are also taken down and the church stays bare without any decoration in preparation for Good Friday to reflect the starkness of Christ's suffering and crucifixion. This custom which is thought to have originated in seventh-century Spain, may also have served a more practical purpose since it gave the local women a chance to give the church a thorough clean before the great celebrations of the Easter weekend.

THE SILENCE OF THE BELLS

On Maundy Thursday the church bells ring out for the last time before Easter Day. Throughout the sad hours of Good Friday and Holy Saturday they remain silent. To explain their silence, one old Catholic legend has it that the bells 'fly to Rome' to make a pilgrimage, visit the Pope and sleep on the roof of St Peter's. As they return, early on Easter morning, they drop Easter eggs into every house in which there are children.

READINGS

John 13:1–15, 34–5
Matthew 26:26–9

A MAUNDY THURSDAY PRAYER

Let us all draw near in fear to the mystical table, and with pure souls let us receive the bread; let us remain at the Master's side, that we may see how he washes the feet of the disciples and wipes them with a towel; and let us do as we have seen, subjecting ourselves to each other and washing one another's feet. For such is the commandment that Christ himself gave to his disciples.
AMEN

An Orthodox Prayer, in *The Oxford Book of Prayer*

Good Friday

RED

After Jesus had taken the vinegar he said, 'It is
accomplished'; and bowing his head he gave up his spirit.
John 19:30

Good Friday is the most solemn day in the whole Christian
Year – the day of Christ's death. On this day, which starts early
in the morning in the gospel accounts, we recollect Jesus'
agony in the garden, his betrayal, his two trials, his flogging
and mockery by the soldiers, his long walk to Golgotha carrying his cross, his crucifixion, his death and his burial.

Since the days of the fourth century, the liturgy for Good
Friday has been filled with a number of special forms of
prayer and worship. More than any other day in the sacred
calendar, Good Friday is a day to meditate upon the suffering of Christ. In most churches this sorrow and reflection is
enacted in different forms of service and rituals – the length
and intensity of which allow us to remain intent upon the
details of Christ's death and the extent of his sacrifice.

The readings for Good Friday are a central part of the
day's services. The gospel reading for the day is the whole of
the Passion Narrative from St John's Gospel which starts
with Jesus' betrayal in the Garden of Gethsemane and ends
with the piercing of his side after his death on the cross. The
other two readings for the day, from Isaiah and the epistle to
the Hebrews, concentrate on the theme of sacrifice.

VENERATION OF THE CROSS

An ancient and traditional ritual which takes place on Good Friday is the Veneration of the Cross. In the earliest Good Friday ceremonies in Jerusalem, it was the custom for the congregation to walk up one by one to kiss or touch a relic of the true cross. This custom became known as the Veneration of the Cross and is still a central ritual in Good Friday services in the Roman Church when people take turns to kiss a crucifix during mass. Throughout the Middle Ages this ritual was also widely practised in England where it was known as 'creeping to the cross', because people would approach the cross on their knees and prostrate themselves before it.

THREE HOURS DEVOTION

Another very popular Good Friday service is the Three Hours Devotion. Although this service has become increasingly common in Protestant Churches, it was originally invented by Peruvian Jesuits in the seventeenth century. The service is built around a series of addresses which reflect upon the seven last words of Jesus from the cross:

'My God, My God, why has thou forsaken me?'
(Matthew 27:46)

'Father, forgive them; for they know not what they do.'
(Luke 23:34)

'Truly, I say to you, today you will be with me
in Paradise.'
(Luke 23:43)

'Father, into thy hands I commit my spirit.'
(Luke 23:46)

'Woman, behold your son.' Then he said to the
disciple, 'Behold your mother.'
(John 19:26–7)

'I thirst.'
(John 19:28)

'It is finished.'
(John 19:30)

Addresses on each of these last words are mingled with
song, prayer, psalms and other readings. To coincide with
the three hours of Jesus' crucifixion, the service is usually
held between 12 noon and 3 o'clock in the afternoon.
This service too has inspired some very beautiful and
mournful sacred music. In 1785 Haydn wrote a series of
seven orchestral interludes to be played between the
seven addresses at this service. The work was commissioned by Cadiz Cathedral and entitled 'The Seven Last
Words of our Saviour From the Cross'. The last of the
seven pieces is famous for evoking the earthquake which
takes place at the moment of Jesus' death in Matthew's
gospel account. A version of the famous 'Stabat Mater' is
also frequently performed on Good Friday. This is a thir-
teenth-century devotional poem about the Virgin Mary's

vigil by the cross at Jesus' crucifixion. The poem's first line, *Stabat Mater Dolorosa*, means 'a grief-stricken mother was standing', and the poem has been set to music by many great composers including Palestrina, Haydn, Rossini, Verdi and Dvorak.

STATIONS OF THE CROSS

The Stations of the Cross is another ritual devotion dating back to the original Holy Week ceremonies of fourth-century Jerusalem. It is widely practised during Lent and Passiontide, but most especially on Good Friday. The so-called 'stations' refer to the fourteen main incidents which happened to Jesus at his Passion and on his final journey through Jerusalem to the cross.

While pilgrims had always retraced the steps of Christ's last journey through the streets of Jerusalem, it was really the Crusaders who developed the Stations of the Cross as we know them today. On their return from the Holy Land, many Crusaders commissioned sculpted reliefs or paintings which recalled particular moments of Christ's last journey and then prayed before them one after the other. In 1342, when the Franciscan monks were given the guardianship of the places of pilgrimage in the Holy Land they greatly encouraged this devotion. From their own monasteries, its practice soon spread to parish churches throughout the world.

Initially, there was great variation in the number and range of incidents remembered, and some churches had up to 30 stations. But in 1731 the number was confirmed at 14 by Pope Clement XII. In recent times however, it has become common to add a fifteenth station which recalls Christ's resurrection. The fourteen stations are:

1 Jesus is condemned to death by Pilate
2 Jesus carries his cross
3 Jesus falls for the first time
4 Jesus meets his mother
5 Jesus is helped by Simon of Cyrene
6 Jesus' face is wiped by Veronica
7 Jesus falls a second time
8 Jesus consoles the women of Jerusalem
9 Jesus falls a third time
10 Jesus is stripped of his garments
11 Jesus is nailed to the cross
12 Jesus dies on the cross
13 Jesus is taken down from the cross
14 Jesus is laid in the tomb

Today these stations are recorded in stonework, paintings or stained glass which are placed in succession round the inside of the church. Individually or in groups, people move from one station to the next praying and meditating before each picture and remembering Christ's particular ordeal at every station. Some stations have also been set up outside in the grounds of monasteries or large houses, or in the streets of villages and towns.

THE 40-HOUR VIGIL

Good Friday is the start of the 40-hour vigil or fast. This vigil lasts for the forty hours from Friday evening until Sunday morning and represents the time between Jesus' death and his resurrection. Throughout this time, the most devoted of people will actually maintain a vigil beside a crucifix or the reserved sacrament which is placed inside a shrine to represent Jesus' tomb. Others will simply keep a fast – albeit a very long one – during this period.

EASTER GARDENS

Good Friday is also an important day for the Easter garden, or Easter grotto, which the children have made for Holy Week. While the crib at Christmas is a model of the manger where Jesus was born, the Easter garden is a model of the tomb and the garden where Jesus was buried. In the evening on Good Friday, it is customary to place a small cross in the tomb to represent Christ's burial. The stone of the tomb may then be rolled tightly shut and remain so until Easter Day.

HOT CROSS BUNS AND FUNERAL PROCESSIONS

Many customs have grown up around Good Friday. Most popular of all being the custom of baking and eating hot cross buns on Good Friday. This custom originated in

England in the fourteenth century where buns with a white cross on them were baked early on Good Friday morning and eaten at breakfast – their warmth from the oven and the spices in their mixture meaning that they were always hot in both temperature and taste.

Further afield in Latin America, it is customary to mount large funeral processions through the streets on Good Friday in which people carry a crucifix of the dead Christ and a statue of the Virgin Mary. These processions move slowly through the towns, not least because for every three steps forward people take, they then take two steps back again to emphasize the tragedy and mourning of the day. In the Syrian Church on Good Friday, people are forbidden to use their traditional daily greeting 'Peace' because this is the word with which Judas greeted Jesus in the Garden of Gethsemane on the morning of the first Good Friday.

Like Christmas Eve, there is also a widely held popular belief that a person who dies on Good Friday will go straight to Paradise to be with Jesus, like the good thief who was crucified next to Jesus (Luke 23:39–43).

READING

John 18:1–19:37

A GOOD FRIDAY PRAYER

O Tree of Calvary,
send your roots deep down
into my heart.
Gather together the soil of my heart,
the sands of my fickleness,
the mud of my desires.
Bind them all together,
O Tree of Calvary,
interlace them with Thy strong roots,
entwine them with the network
of Thy love. AMEN

Prayer of an Indian Christian,
in *Morning, Noon and Night*

Easter

THE GREATEST OF FEASTS

Easter is the greatest of all Christian feasts. St Gregory of Nazianzus said that Easter was 'like the sun among the stars' of the other festivals. It is the very heart of the sacred calendar, around which all other seasons and festivals have sprung to life. And Easter celebrations are the most ancient part of the Christian calendar, going back to the very beginnings of Christianity.

In most languages the word for Easter takes its root from the Hebrew word Pesach meaning Passover – like *Paques* in French and *Pasqua* in Italian. Passover is the great Jewish feast which celebrates the Israelites' Exodus from slavery in Egypt and was the feast Jesus celebrated with his disciples the night before he died. In English however, the word Easter comes from the old English word 'Ost' and the current word 'east' which refer to the direction in which the sun rises. The word has its roots in ancient festivals which celebrated the spring sun and the ancient Saxon Goddess Eostra who was goddess of the dawn of the year. This theme of new light is a central part of the Christian Easter which celebrates the resurrection of Christ's light from the darkness of death and evil – the Son-rise as well as the sunrise.

The Easter Vigil

Very early in the morning on the first day of the week,
they came to the tomb, just as the sun was rising.

Mark 16:2

Easter really gets underway during the night of Holy Saturday. As darkness falls, the mood begins to change from sadness and mourning to expectation and excitement as the Easter Vigil begins. With Sunday, the Easter Vigil is the oldest of all Christian celebrations and dates back to the days of the Apostles themselves. The service traditionally lasts until dawn but these days there are many variations – many of which do not last all night. During the long vigil, people watch, pray and worship, waiting in earnest for the rising of the sun on Easter morning.

A SERVICE FULL OF LIGHT

The Easter Vigil is the great service of light in the Christian Year. For hundreds of years, Christians have celebrated the joy of Christ's resurrection with candles and bonfires throughout Saturday night and the early hours of Easter morning. In the Eastern Church particularly, the night of Holy Saturday is known as 'the night of illumination' and in their Vigil service people are encouraged to make the dark hours of Holy Saturday as bright as day itself. But the Vigil service is not just a celebration of light. It also expresses the Christian's sense of joy and salvation in the sound of bells, words of praise and holy water too.

THE NEW FIRE AND PASCHAL CANDLE

The Vigil service starts with the lighting of the paschal candle. This large candle is traditionally lit from a bonfire outside the church and carried into the church. The custom of an Easter bonfire originated in Ireland in the sixth century. The bonfire was part of a much older pre-Christian springtime ritual which St Patrick imbued with Christian meaning and encouraged its use at the Vigil service. The bonfire gives off great heat as well as light, and so symbolizes the warmth of God which quickens the earth once again at Easter, thawing a dormant world and bringing it to life. In the cold northern climates, symbols of light and heat find an equal place at the heart of the Easter mystery. For if Christ's resurrection enlightens our souls, it certainly also warms our hearts. Fireworks are also used to celebrate the Easter vigil in many countries today and light up the skies around the Vigil service.

Once inside the church, the candle is used to light all the smaller candles held by members of the congregation, so that the whole church gradually fills with light. The paschal candle itself is then set up in the church and kept alight for the full 50 days of Eastertide. In some churches, it is customary to put five grains of incense in the paschal candle to recall the five wounds of Christ.

During the Middle Ages, paschal candles became an art form in themselves. They were frequently huge and had the date of the year elaborately carved around them. One paschal candle in Salisbury Cathedral was 11 metres high while another in Westminster Abbey weighed 740 kilos. In times when family homes were lit and warmed by naked flame, people would extinguish the lights and fires in their homes on Holy Saturday. After the Vigil they would then take their Easter candles home with them and rekindle their lights and their hearth fire with its small flame, lit directly from the paschal candle.

WORDS OF JOY AND THE PEAL OF BELLS

With the church filled with light there are a number of readings from Scripture, and the special words of rejoicing which have remained unheard during Lent are spoken once again. The Gloria – which has not been said or sung since the beginning of Lent – is proclaimed or sung again. And the bells which have been silent since Maundy Thursday ring out once more to announce the coming of Easter. Then, after the Epistle has been read, the joyful word Alleluia is said again – the great word of triumph and rejoicing which has been left unsaid throughout the solemn days of Lent.

HOLY WATER AND BAPTISMAL VOWS

In the Middle Ages, the Easter Vigil was the service at which the catechumens would have been brought into the church robed in white and baptized at midnight after their lengthy preparation. Today, the Vigil service is still an important occasion for adult baptism and a service in which all Christians renew their baptismal vows. In many churches the congregation is also sprinkled with the newly blessed holy water from the font.

READINGS

Matthew 27:57–66
John 2:18–22

Easter Day

WHITE OR GOLD

On the first day of the week the disciples went to the tomb,
and they found the stone rolled away from the tomb. Alleluia!
Luke 24:1–2

With sunrise on Sunday morning, the Easter Vigil passes into Easter Day itself. This is the day of Jesus' resurrection and the most precious and joyful day in the whole Christian Year.

THE EASTER EUCHARIST

In most churches the Eucharist is obligatory on Easter Day and the Easter service is traditionally an extremely happy occasion when communion or mass is celebrated in a spirit of great gladness. At last, after the solemn weeks of Lent, ministers and priests put on their most splendid white or gold vestments – the dazzling colours of the sun. The church is once more filled with the scent and colour of flowers. Bright altar cloths are spread over the altar, and paintings, sculptures and crosses are uncovered once again. To further symbolize the resurrection it is customary for priest and congregation to pray standing up on Easter Day, and not to kneel down. This is a sign that we are risen with Christ and that it is too joyful a day to be bent low.

EASTER LAUGHTER

But if the morning Eucharist is celebrated with gladness, the evening service is traditionally celebrated with nothing short of glee. In England, throughout the Middle Ages and up until the eighteenth century, it was the custom for the priest or minister to fill his evening sermon with jokes and stories to make the people roar with laughter after the long seriousness of Lent and the sorrow of Holy Week. And it is not just people who are happy on Easter Day, for legend has it that the sun itself jumps for joy three times to celebrate the resurrection as it rises on Easter morning. Not surprisingly perhaps, these jumps are hard to detect and are supposedly best observed indirectly, by watching the sunrise reflected in a pail of water or a window.

BONNETS, PROMENADES AND PARDONS

There are many popular customs associated with Easter Day. Paraded in their clean white robes, the catechumens were not the only ones to wear new clothes at Easter. For centuries, people have put on a new outfit on Easter Day and the custom of wearing a new Easter bonnet was but the tip of an iceberg. New dresses, trousers, coats, jackets and shoes were always the norm for those who could afford them on Easter Day.

Having gone to the expense of buying or making these new clothes, it made sense to show them off. The Easter walk or promenade when people paraded their new outfits through the fields or town was traditionally a great event on Easter Day. Like other great feasts it was always customary to hold open house on Easter Day and to visit and be visited by one's relatives and neighbours. The Easter bells are also a resounding feature of Easter Day. They would often ring all day to celebrate the end of the fast and the joy of Easter. Today's ringing however, is more measured.

Because of Pilate's release of Barabbas in the gospel account of Jesus' trial, and the mercy Jesus himself showed to the good thief who was crucified beside him, Easter Day is also a traditional time for amnesties and pardons. In many countries, the release of non-dangerous criminals is often announced at Easter. In many national and international peace negotiations, political prisoners have also been released at Easter.

EGGS, LAMB AND EASTER BUNNIES

The most common Easter customs which survive today are the ones concerned with food. Indeed, these have probably always been the most popular. For after the long days of the Lenten fast, Easter Day and Easter Week is a time of great feasting.

Easter eggs are the most famous Easter food. In pre-Christian festivals of the spring equinox, eggs were always a symbol of spring. The sight of a living creature emerging from a still, apparently inert object was always cherished as a graphic example of the miracle of new life. In Christian times, this wonderful symbol was eagerly taken up and

Christianized. The enclosed shell of the egg came to remind people of the sealed tomb from which the risen
Christ, like the new chick, emerged triumphant. From early
in Christian history, eggs were painted and given as gifts on
Easter Day. Red is a favourite colour of such painted eggs to
symbolize the blood of Christ. Many traditional Easter
games have also grown up involving eggs. Easter egg hunts
and egg rolling are still the most popular today. In the USA,
the President still has an egg-rolling competition on the
White House lawn every Easter.

Easter lamb and Easter ham are two other favourite
foods of the Easter feast. Lamb is the traditional food of the
Jewish feast of Passover and is what Jesus would have eaten
with his disciples at the Last Supper. Because of his own
passover sacrifice for us, Jesus is often referred to as the
Lamb of God or the Paschal Lamb. Lamb is therefore the
centrepiece of the Easter feast. And in Christian mythology
a lamb is regarded as the supreme symbol of innocence
and an especially sacred animal. Because it is such a holy
animal, it has always been believed that a lamb is the one
shape which the Devil can never take to disguise himself. It
is still considered good luck to see a lamb in the fields on
Easter Day. Ham is another great feasting food in many
parts of the world in cultures where the pig has been a traditional symbol of good luck. And in Europe and Ireland
special Easter bread is also baked for the Easter feast.

The Easter bunny – who, an improbable legend has it,
lays the Easter eggs – is another feature of popular Easter
culture in Europe and the USA where the fields are filled
with newborn rabbits at this time. The rabbit itself has

never acquired a particularly Christian significance. Its place in Easter legend stems from when the hare was regarded as a sacred animal in pre-Christian times and played an important role in springtime festivals.

THE SUMMIT OF THE YEAR

Easter Day is the summit of the Christian Year. Knowledge of Christ's resurrection is the highest point of Christian experience from where faith views the horizon of God's purpose clearly for the first time. The fact that Christ is risen shows that God will never leave us, but that He is always with us, making a new thing from the midst of conflict, suffering and death. And Easter also tells us that we will always be with God. For just as Christ is risen, so too can we expect to be risen with him to the eternal life of which he spoke on earth.

READINGS

Matthew 28:1–10
John 20:1–10
Mark 16:1–8

Eastertide – the Season of Easter

And Mary Magdalene went and said to
the disciples, 'I have seen the Lord.'
John 20:18

Eastertide is the happiest time of the Christian Year and lasts for fifty days from Easter Day until the Feast of Pentecost. During this time above all others, we celebrate Christ's presence amongst us.

THE VIBRANCY OF NEW LIFE

In the northern hemisphere, the season of Easter coincides with springtime and the beginning of summer, a time when the world around us is steeped in light and abounds with new life. The sun rises earlier each morning and sets later each night. The trees are in bud and the flowers are in bloom. In the animal world, birds are nesting, chicks are hatching and curious ducklings are skidding about on the rivers. The fields are full of tottering lambs, hesitant calves and hordes of scampering young rabbits.

If Christmas is a time to celebrate the coming of Christ's light into a dark world, Easter is the time to rejoice at the triumph and pervasion of that light and the power of God to bring about new life. It is a season which affirms the irrepressibility of life and the unstoppable nature of God's revelation of love and renewal in Christ.

GLORIOUS DAYS

The first 40 days of Easter up until Ascension Day are known as the 'Forty Glorious Days' when the risen Christ was still with the disciples in bodily form and appeared before them regularly. These glorious days are the time of confirmation and reassurance when the risen Christ is still recognizable and present to the disciples, and continues to comfort and teach them in person. It is the season of proof, and of gradual realization and understanding. Passiontide and Holy Week were the season in which we felt our loss and sadness at the suffering of the earthly Jesus. Eastertide is the season in which we, like the disciples, make sense of what has happened and realize the magnitude of our gain. Our eyes are opened, and what we thought was the end, we recognize as the beginning. Christ is with us for ever.

EASTER WEEK

Eastertide starts with Easter Week, the week after Easter Sunday. Each day of Easter Week is a feast and church services shine with the liturgical colours of white and gold. Day by day, the gospel readings tell of how the risen Jesus appeared to his disciples. On Monday we hear how Christ joined two of the disciples on the road to Emmaus, and how they did not recognize him until they invited him to supper where he blessed the bread for them and vanished. Tuesday's reading tells of Christ's sudden appearance before the disciples and how he eats grilled fish before their eyes. Wednesday's gospel tells the famous story of Doubting Thomas who has to feel Jesus' wounds before he is prepared to believe in the risen Christ. Thursday tells how Jesus met the disciples by the Sea of Tiberias, how he called to them as they were fishing, miraculously gave them a huge catch, and then cooked breakfast for them on the beach. Listening to these stories and the others which follow in the rest of Eastertide, Christ's risen presence reverberates among us as at no other time of year.

THE CHARGE TO PETER

Eastertide is also the time of organization and delegation when the risen Christ sets up an earthly institution, the Church, which will represent him and minister to the world. On the last two Sundays in Easter the readings recall Jesus' charge to Peter to take responsibility for the disciples and his followers. He is instructed to 'feed my lambs' and 'tend my sheep'. Jesus also tells his disciples of the coming of the Holy Spirit who will guide them and the church for the rest of time.

READINGS

Easter Week:	Monday	Luke 24:13–35
	Tuesday	Luke 24:36–49
	Wednesday	John 20:24–31
	Thursday	John 21:1–14
	Friday	John 21:15–17
	Saturday	John 21:20–25

Easter 1   John 20:19 –29 or John 6:32– 40
Easter 2   Luke 24:13 –35 or John 10:7– 16
Easter 3   John 21:15 –22 or John 11:17– 27
Easter 4   John 21:15 –22 or John 14:1– 11
Easter 5   John 16:25 –33 or John 16:12– 24

TWO PRAYERS FOR EASTER

Risen Lord Jesus, as Mary Magdalene met you in the garden
on the morning of your resurrection,
so may we meet you today and every day:
speak to us as you spoke to her;
reveal yourself as the living Lord;
renew our hope and kindle our joy;
and send us to share the good news with others. AMEN

From *Lent, Holy Week and Easter*, Church of England, Church House
Publishing/Cambridge University Press/SPCK, 1986

May the light of Christ,
rising in glory,
scatter the darkness of our heart and mind.

From the Roman Missal, *The Oxford Book of Prayer*

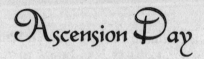

Ascension Day

WHITE OR GOLD

Jesus lifted up his hands: and, while he blessed his disciples, he parted from them.
Luke 24:50–51

Ascension Day remembers the risen Jesus' ascension to heaven from the top of a mountain in Galilee. It comes forty days after Easter Day, on the Thursday of the sixth week after Easter, and so marks the end of the forty glorious days of Jesus' resurrection appearances.

A COMMAND AND A PROMISE

Before leaving them, Jesus gives his disciples one final instruction and makes one last promise. His command is 'to make disciples of all the nations; baptize them in the name of the Father, Son and Holy Spirit, and teach them to observe all the commands I gave you' (Matthew 28:19–20a). After he gives them his blessing he also makes a promise: 'Know that I am with you always; yes, to the end of time' (Matthew 28:20b).

Ascension Day is a time to recall this command and this promise. Peter's charge to look after the Church is now matched by the Church's charge to go out and minister to the whole world. In his last words, Christ makes plain again that Christianity is a faith for everyone and that the disciples and the Church have a duty to all peoples. And Christ's last promise makes it known that we do not minister alone, but that Christ will be with us always, in everything we do and everywhere we go.

AN APOSTOLIC FEAST

Ascension Day is one of the oldest and greatest feast days of the Christian Year. It dates back to the time of the Apostles themselves and is remembered by St Luke at the very beginning of the Acts of the Apostles. Christ's ascension is therefore one of the original four great moments of the Christian faith (along with the Passion, the resurrection and the coming of the Holy Spirit) which have been celebrated by Christians from the earliest times. These four feasts stand tall as the great pillars of the Christian calendar, around which all other feasts and seasons have positioned themselves over the centuries.

RITUAL HEIGHTS

Great heights and hilltops inevitably play a major part in most Ascension Day customs. Processions to a holy hill for services and picnics are still a common way to celebrate Ascension Day in many Christian cultures. There is also an ancient tradition of incorporating the church roof into a wide range of vertigo-inducing rites. For example, as the congregation stands waiting below with their arms raised to heaven, a crucifix is hoisted up through a hole in the church roof or held on high from the spire to re-enact Christ's ascension. In many countries, it is also the custom to eat a bird on Ascension Day, like a pigeon, pheasant or partridge, in memory of the fact that Christ flew up to heaven like a bird.

READINGS

Matthew 28:16–20
Acts 1:1–11

AN ASCENSION DAY PRAYER

O God,
you withdraw from our sight
that you may be known by our love;
help us to enter the cloud
where you are hidden,
and surrender all our certainty
to the darkness of faith
in Jesus Christ, AMEN

From *All Desires Known*, Janet Morley

PENTECOST AND TRINITY

The Holy Spirit

The Season of Pentecost and Trinity

GREEN

If the Spirit is the source of life,
let the Spirit also direct our course.

Galatians 5:25

The Feasts of Pentecost, Trinity Sunday and Corpus Christi mark the beginning of the long season of ordinary time which lasts for 23 weeks between Pentecost and the end of the Christian Year. The two great cycles of Christmas and Easter are complete. We now pass the rest of the year in so-called 'ordinary time' without any special long periods of penitence, preparation or feasting.

The predominant liturgical colour for this long season is green. The violet, blue and black of the penitential seasons are behind us. The red, white and gold are used only for the remaining saints' days and feast days in the year. For the next 22 Sundays the altar cloths and priestly vestments will be the gentle green of ordinary time.

The religious temper of this season is gentler too. The great events of the incarnation, crucifixion and resurrection are fulfilled. We have re-enacted them again, been challenged by them, and rewarded by them too. The first half of the Christian Year has been about the discovery of hard truths and the experience of great joys. The second half is more mundane. It is much less a time of discovery. Instead, we now settle down to carry on our lives in the light of what we have come to know. This is the season of home truths, when we work out the social consequences of Christ's teaching and see what it means to put our faith into practice in the community where we live.

ORDINARY TIME, EVERYDAY PROBLEMS

While this is a gentler season, it is nevertheless a season which challenges us morally and socially. Pentecost/Trinity is the season when we learn if we can love one another in ordinary time, without all the social props of feasts and festivals. Precisely because it is so very ordinary, this season challenges us spiritually too. Over the course of its long weeks, we will see whether we can continue to nurture our faith without all the ritual disciplines of holy days, fasting, vigils and celebrations. We will have to find a way to discover holiness in our everyday lives and to be ordinarily religious for a change.

Many of the readings for this season make us think about our attitudes to our family, our neighbours and those in authority over us. They prompt us to think about serving the community, forgiving others, loving our enemies, and not being materialistic. Above all, they make us think about right and wrong. We hear many of Jesus' parables between now and the end of the year. In these stories, Jesus often gives us a choice: to be like a wise virgin or a foolish virgin; a good Samaritan or an uncaring priest; a pharisee or a publican. The choices Jesus puts to us are the choices of everyday life, the issues of ordinary time. Our decisions in these matters are the acid test of our faith. It is our outward actions towards our neighbours and our world which count in the end. The number of fasts we make, vigils we keep or festivals we celebrate is as nothing if we do not love one another. This conviction is at the heart of Jesus' teaching and is the main challenge of ordinary time and the season of the Spirit.

A PRAYER FOR ORDINARY TIME

Lord of all power and might,
the author of all good things;
graft in our hearts the love of your name,
increase in us true religion,
nourish in us all goodness,
and of your great mercy keep us in the same;
through Jesus Christ our Lord. AMEN

Collect for the 17th Sunday after Pentecost,
Alternate Service Book

Pentecost or Whitsun

And suddenly a sound came from heaven like the rush of a
mighty wind, and it filled all the house where they were sitting.
And there appeared to them tongues as of fire, distributed and
resting on each one of them.
Acts 2:2–3

The Feast of Pentecost celebrates the coming of the Holy Spirit upon the disciples ten days after Jesus' ascension. It brings the mysteries of Eastertide to a dramatic and wonderful culmination, and sees the paschal candle lit for the last time. In the northern hemisphere, Pentecost is the great midsummer festival, a particularly invigorating time when scents and colours are at their peak, and the hedgerows hum with birds and bees. It is a time of full bloom when the human soul itself brims over with excitement and a strange feeling that everything is possible. It is the time of the Holy Spirit – the third person of the Trinity.

THE BIRTHDAY OF THE CHURCH

If Ascension Day left the disciples wondering, not for the first time, what was going to happen next, then the extraordinary events of Pentecost left them in no doubt. Jesus' Ascension Day promise that he will always be with them comes true and they are given new powers with which to carry out his last commandment and take the Gospel to the whole world. Suddenly, the disciples are able to go out into the streets and to speak boldly of the good news they have encountered in Christ's life, death and resurrection. In an instant, they have both the understanding and the strength with which to begin their mission.

Because of this, the Feast of Pentecost is known as 'the birthday of the Church'. It was by the power of the Holy Spirit that Peter and the other Apostles were able to leave the confines of the upper room and go out into the seething city to spread the word. Pentecost and the arrival of the Spirit turned their lives inside out. What they had experienced inwardly, they now witnessed outwardly to others. During the fifty days of Eastertide, they had stayed huddled together, often confused and afraid, while their understanding of Christ's resurrection gradually dawned. But now a new sense of clarity and courage forced itself upon them and they spread out to journey through the whole world. It was now the time for others to be bewildered and amazed, confounded by the conviction of the Apostles and their ability to speak in every language.

TASTING THE FIRST FRUITS

Pentecost is a Greek word meaning fiftieth. In Jesus' day, it was the name given to the season between the Jewish Feast of Passover and the Feast of Weeks which celebrated the 'first fruits' of the spring harvest. This feast took place 50 days, or seven weeks, after Passover. It was one of the great feasts of the Jewish year and was the reason why so many Jewish people from so many parts of the world were visiting Jerusalem at the time of the first Christian Pentecost. In the Christian calendar therefore, Pentecost comes 50 days after Easter and celebrates the gifts of the Holy Spirit.

Preaching at Pentecost in Antioch in the early fifth century, St John of Chrysostom recognized the significance of the spiritual harvest celebrated at this time when he said: 'Today we have arrived at the peak of all blessings, we have reached the capital of feasts, we have obtained the very fruit of our Lord's promise.' In the gifts of the Holy Spirit, Christians taste the first fruits of the Kingdom of Heaven of which Jesus spoke. This is the Spirit which works in us always to wake us to God's calling and refresh us with new life. The same Spirit which gives us wisdom and understanding, guides us towards right judgment, comforts us in our distress, fills our hearts with joy and wonder, and gives us courage.

WHITSUN, WIT AND WITNESS

In English, Pentecost is also known as Whitsunday, and the three days around the feast (Saturday, Sunday and Monday) are known as Whitsuntide or Whitsun. The word Whitsun comes from the time when Pentecost, like Easter, was an important time for baptism. As at Easter, the new catechumens would all wear white clothes at the Feast of Pentecost and so it was called 'White Sunday'.

The English language encourages other associations to

be made between the word Whitsun and the events of Pentecost. Many a preacher has related the origins of Whitsun to the day when the Apostles received the 'wit' and wisdom of the Holy Spirit which enabled them to go forth and bear 'witness' to the world.

THE RED FEAST

Despite Whitsun's associations with the colour white in Britain, the liturgical colour of Pentecost is actually red, instead of white or gold. This is very unusual for a great and joyous feast day, and is intended to signify the colour of the tongues of fire which descended upon the Apostles in the upper room. Because of this, Pentecost is known as the Red Feast in several parts of Europe. In many places, the red peony also flowers around this time and is known as the 'Rose of Pentecost'.

WHITE DOVE, MIGHTY WIND AND WILD GOOSE

The most ancient and traditional Christian symbol of the Holy Spirit is the white dove. This stems from the gospel stories of Jesus' baptism in which Jesus saw 'the Spirit descending upon him like a dove' as he emerged from the waters of the river Jordan (Mark 1:10). The rituals and customs of Pentecost have often involved the dove in a variety of ways, some taking the symbolism more literally than others.

In many a Christian home, it was common to have a

carved wooden dove which would be displayed promi-
nently during Pentecost as a reminder of the Holy Spirit.
Throughout the centuries, the Pentecost story has also
been dramatized in church services, and still is in many
places. In the Middle Ages, a large circular board would be
lowered through the hole in the church roof, known as the
'Holy Ghost Hole', at the moment during the service when
the priest or choir sang 'Come, Holy Spirit'. On this board
was a painting of a white dove against a sky-blue back-
ground with golden rays around it to symbolize divinity. In
some churches mere paintings were not enough. At services in the great French cathedrals, great flocks of turtle
doves were released high in the vaulted ceilings and left to
fly freely through the building.

Similarly dramatic were the ritual representations of the
tongues of fire. The most common symbol for this manifestation of the Holy Spirit was flowers, particularly red rose
petals. These too were released from high up in the church
and showered upon the worshippers below. And dramatiza-
tions were not confined to visual effects alone. Trumpets
and hissing choirboys imitated the noise of the Holy Spirit
which sounded like a 'mighty wind'. Today, members of the
congregation, especially children, are still encouraged to
join in to recreate the noise of the rushing wind.

In many countries, people fly kites at Pentecost to celebrate the mighty wind. Kite flying is a powerful symbol of the
workings of the Holy Spirit upon the human soul. Clinging
to the end of a kite line on a gusty day is an effective way to
feel the power of the wind, and so to reflect upon the power
of the Spirit. Watching the kite soaring to great heights one

minute and then swooping low over the land the next, focuses the mind (and the arm muscles!) on the power, elation and freedom of the human soul when inspired by the Spirit.

The wild goose was the symbol of the Holy Spirit in ancient Celtic Christianity, and still is in many Celtic communities in Britain and Ireland today. This large, migrating bird well represents the powerful aspect of the Holy Spirit which can move us and uproot us from the security of our daily lives. As the Apostles discovered soon after Pentecost, the Holy Spirit can lead us far from home and take us into unfamiliar territory. If we follow its flight it can challenge us deeply and change us profoundly.

The notion of a journey, spiritual or physical, is integral to Pentecost. Pilgrimages often start at Whitsun. King Arthur's knights set out on their great quest for the Holy Grail at Whitsun and many pilgrims start their long journeys at this time. The adventurous, journeying side of the Spirit is an important one to remember at Pentecost. Ancient Celtic Christians like St Patrick and St Brendan valued a wandering, questing faith as much as a resolute and confrontational one. Their old Celtic Church described those Christians whose calling was a wandering one as 'green martyrs', and called 'red martyrs' those whose destiny was to suffer for their faith.

BLOWN TOGETHER

If the Holy Spirit can set us on a journey, it also has the power to bind us to one another and breathe a sense of community into our lives. At the end of a journey there is often a gathering. Whitsun is a famous time for large open-air gatherings, full of music, games and dance. In England, Whitsun is the time of Morris dancing, well dressing, miracle plays and Whitsun Ale. Even today, the great music festivals, race meetings and other sporting events often occur around this time. In Scotland, June, July and August is the time for the gathering of the clans and the famous highland games. The British Army gathers too in June. In London, at the Trooping of the Colour, the army parades in all its splendour in front of the Queen. This ancient ceremony was originally an occasion to rally all soldiers together and show them the 'colours', or banner, which they would fight under. They would then be able to recognize it quickly and gather round it in the heat of battle.

Whitsun is also the time of the elderflower. This white whitsun flower appears in abundance in England at this time. In recent years elderflower cordial has been rediscovered by many people. It has become increasingly popular as a summer drink, a refreshing non-alcoholic alternative to the more heady Whitsun Ale.

READINGS

Acts 2:1–21
John 14:15–26

PENTECOST PRAYERS

O God, the Holy Ghost,
come to us, and among us:
come as the wind and cleanse us;
come as the fire, and burn;
come as the dew, and refresh;
convict, convert and consecrate
many hearts and lives
to our great good
and thy greater glory,
and this we ask in Jesus Christ's sake. AMEN

By George Appleton, from *In His Name*, Lutterworth Press, 1978

Spirit of energy and change,
in whose power Jesus was anointed
to be the hope of the nations;
be poured out also upon us
without reserve or distinction,
that we may have confidence and strength
to plant your justice on the earth,
through Jesus Christ, AMEN

From *All Desires Known*, Janet Morley

Trinity Sunday

WHITE OR GOLD

Glory be to the Father, and to the Son
and to the Holy Spirit:
as it was in the beginning, is now,
and shall be for ever.

The first Sunday after Pentecost is Trinity Sunday which is the feast day of the Holy Trinity. This feast is different from all others in the *temporale* of the Christian calendar because it does not celebrate a historical event from the life of Christ or the Apostles. Instead, it celebrates the theological doctrine, or religious truth, of the Trinity: that the one God is three persons, Father, Son and Holy Spirit.

Celebrating this truth, Trinity Sunday draws our attention to a profound aspect of the Christian faith which the sacred year to date has revealed to us slowly but surely. The gradual unfolding of the gospel events throughout the ritual year is the gradual unfolding of the mystery of the Trinity. The gospel stories lead us to know that we meet God as three persons in our religious life. On Trinity Sunday we celebrate this knowledge which is at the heart of Christ's teaching and which the Christian Church guards as one of its most precious beliefs.

GOD'S DAY

The fact that Trinity Sunday is not tied to a specific historical event is refreshing. This is a day when we don't have to remember any particular stories or rituals. Instead, it is a day when we can simply put all our energies into celebrating God. Like the birthday of a friend or relation, Trinity Sunday is a day which is dedicated to rejoicing, purely and simply, in a person's very being. But today that person is God. As we rejoice, we praise the diversity of God's person as we have come to know it – as Father, Son and Holy Spirit.

THE HIGHEST PRAISE

Trinity Sunday is about praising God in the highest, an uninhibited glorying in the sheer greatness of God. So far during the Christian Year, we have celebrated God as he has drawn near to us in the events of Christ's life on earth. Today we praise the majesty and eternity of God who is the God of heaven as well as earth. We praise the God who stands outside time as well as the God who acts within it. It is a day to offer praise as far as the very limits of our minds and imaginings will take us, and then beyond that to the centre of a universe and a creation which we do not fully understand.

THREE IN ONE

A feast day for the Holy Trinity was first celebrated in Europe during the tenth century but was not placed officially within the Western Christian calendar until 1334 when Pope John XXII fixed it for the Sunday after Pentecost. The doctrine of the Trinity has been one of the most bitterly contested of all doctrines in the Christian Church. It has also been the Christian doctrine least understood and most misrepresented by people from other faiths. Such controversy is a sign of the importance and also the difficulty of a doctrine which has always been more easily expressed in symbols than in words.

In their search for symbols of the Trinity, Christians have been inspired by nature as well as by their own designs. The Greek word 'trinity' was first used in the third century by Tertullian, one of the early Church's greatest theologians. He gave the example of a tree to illustrate the mystery that God is three persons. Tertullian suggested that, while a tree is all one substance, God the Father can be compared to its root, the Son to its branches, and the Spirit to its fruit. This image of a tree was meant to show how God is not divided but extended into three persons. One of the best known natural symbols of the Trinity comes from Ireland. It is the shamrock. Like the three-leafed clover, the shamrock is a family of wild plants which is easily identified by its three leaves extending from a single stem. For centuries, ordinary people have found that this simple plant illustrates the Trinity more clearly than the many lofty words of theologians.

People have also used geometry and architecture to

represent the mystery of the Trinity in more geometric form. A common symbol of the Trinity is a triangle, sometimes with a single eye in the middle of it and surrounded by gold rays. The lines of the triangle illustrate the equal relation of the three persons of the Trinity while the eye symbolizes omniscience and the rays represent divinity. Trinitarian symbolism often appears in church architecture too, where pillars or arches are frequently constructed in groups of three, and joined together to express the unity of the Trinity. In a more routine way, Christian belief in the Trinity is expressed in the ancient custom of using the first three fingers of the right hand when crossing oneself at the blessing. This custom, mentioned by St Augustine as an ancient custom already in the fourth century, continues to this day.

PROTECTION FROM PLAGUE

In many European cities, the Holy Trinity was especially called upon in times of plague and epidemic, perhaps in the hope of maximum divine intervention on such calamitous occasions. New churches were dedicated to the Holy Trinity in time of plague and special pillars were built in honour of the Trinity when an epidemic had abated. Vienna has eleven so-called Trinity Columns which stand in prominent city squares.

FLOWERS AND FRIENDSHIP

In the Russian Church, the Feast of the Holy Trinity is traditionally a festival for young women who celebrate their friendships and their hopes for the future at Trinity. On the Thursday before Trinity Sunday, all young girls would go secretly into the woods together. There they would decorate a birch tree of their choice with garlands of wild flowers, into which they would weave a wish. They would then sing and dance together and, in pairs, renew their vows of lasting friendship by kissing through the garlands. Three days later on Trinity Sunday itself, they would return to the woods to inspect their trees and their garlands. If their garlands were still intact their wishes would come true.

READING

John 14:8–17

A PRAYER FOR TRINITY SUNDAY

O God our mystery,
you bring us to life,
call us to freedom,
and move between us with love.
May we so participate
in the dance of your Trinity,
that our lives may resonate with you,
now and forever, AMEN

From *All Desires Known,* Janet Morley

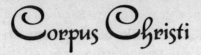

Corpus Christi

CORPUS CHRISTI

Take, eat; this is my body.
Matthew 26:26

The Feast of Corpus Christi is a celebration of the sacrament of the Holy Eucharist, and takes place on the Thursday after Trinity Sunday, ten days after Pentecost.

Corpus Christi is a Latin phrase which means 'the body of Christ'. While the Roman Catholic Church always celebrates Corpus Christi, it remains optional in most Protestant Churches. This is because it is seen as a duplication of Maundy Thursday, the day in Holy Week when we remember the Last Supper and the institution of the Eucharist. The reluctance of some Protestant Churches to celebrate Corpus Christi is also due to their reservations about giving Holy Communion so central a place in worship and liturgy.

FROM DREAM TO REALITY

The Feast of Corpus Christi is not an ancient feast but emerged in the thirteenth century when a Belgian nun, St Juliana, was puzzled by a recurring dream. In her dream, Juliana kept seeing a brilliant full moon shining down upon the earth, but the moon was spoilt by a black spot which blotted out a section of its surface. After being troubled by this dream for many years, she received a vision in which Christ interpreted it to her. He explained that the moon was the Christian Year and that the black spot represented the sole imperfection of that year: the lack of any special feast to celebrate the sacrament of the Holy Eucharist.

From this moment on, Juliana began to suggest that the Church inaugurate a feast for the Eucharist. One of her close friends and advisors, the Bishop of Liège, was soon convinced of her vision and ardently in favour of a new feast day. By chance (or more probably by divine providence!) he became the next pope, and as Pope Urban IV he introduced the Feast of Corpus Christi. The feast was first celebrated in 1264, six years after Juliana's death, and Urban commissioned the great scholar (and later Saint) Thomas Aquinas to compose the special prayers and hymns for the services on Corpus Christi.

A JOYFUL REMEMBRANCE

Behind Juliana's wish for a feast for the Eucharist lay the desire to celebrate this most special sacrament with gladness. Maundy Thursday was felt to be too sad a time to express the heartfelt joy at the transformation which people experience in the Eucharist. To complement Maundy Thursday's commemoration, another feast was needed at a more joyful time of year. This would allow the Church to celebrate how Christ's gift of the Eucharist has revived and comforted Christians in every generation since the Last Supper.

In the 700 years since the first Feast of Corpus Christi, millions of Christians have found that the Feast meets this need. In many parts of the world the feast has become one of the most popular feasts in the calendar. In the United States, two cities, Corpus Christi in Texas and Sacramento in California, were named in honour of the Feast and the Eucharist it celebrates.

CHRIST IS WITH US

Coming as it does at the height of the Christian Year after Pentecost and Trinity, the Feast of Corpus Christi is an opportunity to rejoice in the sacrament in which we most readily draw near to Christ himself. The feast is an occasion to celebrate that Christ, the second person of the Trinity, is with us still. After the parting of Ascension Day, the greeting of the Spirit at Pentecost, and the celebration of God on Trinity Sunday, we now remind ourselves that Christ is here amongst us always. In the Eucharist he has left us an extraordinary remembrance of himself, and when we meet in communion we do so in the knowledge that 'whenever two or three are gathered together in my name, there am I in the midst of them' (Matthew 18:20).

PAGEANTS AND PLAYS

Very soon after its inauguration, the Feast of Corpus Christi took on many of the summer festivities which were naturally taking place in Europe at this time of year and made them its own. Some of the most dramatic and colourful pageants and processions took place at Corpus Christi and still do in many Roman Catholic countries round the world. The blessed sacrament itself is processed round the church or through the streets after the morning Mass, with people kneeling by the roadside as it passes by them.

But Corpus Christi was most famous for its pageants and miracle plays. These medieval plays were a way of teaching Bible stories at a time when Latin was still the official language of the Church. Strange as it may seem, ordinary people seldom heard the words of the Bible in their own language and so these plays were an engaging and amusing way to retell the stories. At Corpus Christi plays were often acted out using an elaborate cart as a stage which was decorated with flowers and drapes. The carts would roll through the town as part of the procession with the actors paraded in costume, cavorting and heckling from the top. When the procession arrived in the town centre or the piece of common land set aside for the festivities, the plays would begin. Several plays would be put on one after the other and performed at several different places in the town during the day. The English city of Chester was particularly famous for its Corpus Christi plays. A cycle of 24 different plays was annually performed here in a number of different parts of the city.

The plays were usually on biblical themes with a lot of singing as well as acting. Most were a lively mix of morality and high farce, and so were educational as well as entertaining. In medieval England, the Corpus Christi plays were often put on by particular groups of craftsmen or labourers who often exploited a biblical theme in common with their trade. Sheep shearers performed plays about the shepherds and the nativity. Water-carriers put on a play about Noah and the flood. Nail-makers acted scenes related to the crucifixion. Bakers would make play on the theme of Corpus Christi itself: the Eucharist and the Last Supper. To this day, a tradition of outdoor theatre in streets, gardens and cloisters continues in the summer months around Corpus Christi.

A SEAL OF FAITH AND UNDERSTANDING

The three great feasts of Pentecost, Trinity Sunday and Corpus Christi, coming as they do within 10 days of each other, mark the end of the most intense half of the liturgical year. In quick succession, we celebrate our certainty of the different ways in which God maintains his presence amongst us as Father, Son and Holy Spirit. These three holy days act like a seal which stamps the first part of the Christian Year, showing that we have understood the great events we have relived in the sacred year to date. What has been laid out before us in history, in the gospels and in the Church's ritual is now impressed firmly on our hearts. The very fact that we can celebrate Pentecost, Trinity Sunday and Corpus Christi with such joy shows how far we have come from those first dark days of Advent when all was expectation but nothing was made known. All then was hope and uncertainty. All now is faith and joy.

READING

John 6:53-8

A CORPUS CHRISTI PRAYER

Be present, be present, O Lord Jesus, thou good High Priest, as thou wast in the midst of thy disciples, and make thyself known to us in the breaking of the bread, who livest and reignest with the Father and the Holy Spirit, one God world without end. AMEN

The Prayer of the Presence: Church of South India,
in *Morning, Noon and Night*

Nativity of The Blessed Virgin Mary

WHITE

Behold, your Mother!
John 19:27

8 September celebrates the birth of the Virgin Mary. This is a very ancient feast which originated in Jerusalem and was also an occasion to honour Mary's parents, St Anne and St Joachim. By the seventh century, devotion to the feast had spread west to the Roman Church.

THE PATTERN OF FAITH

The feast celebrating Mary's birth is one of the three great Marian feasts which recognize the sanctity of Mary's own person and not just her practical role in the gospel events. The so-called vocational feasts like Candlemas, the Annunciation and the Visitation remember what Mary did by virtue of being Jesus' mother. The personal feasts celebrate her particular personal qualities, which together with her role as the mother of God, make her the greatest of all saints. And the quality which is most outstanding in the Virgin Mary is her faith.

A PONDERING HEART

Mary's is not just a simple faith which accepts and believes. It is also a faith which considers and develops. While Mary believed easily, she also reflected on what she believed. Her encounter with Gabriel at the Annunciation (Luke 1:26–38) shows that she 'considered in her mind' (29) the things she was experiencing. At the same time she was able to say 'let it be to me according to your word' (38). Similarly, after the birth of Jesus and the adoration of the shepherds, Mary 'kept all these things, pondering them in her heart' (Luke 2:19).

In her faith, the Virgin Mary is thus the perfect pattern for our own faith. Like Mary's, a healthy faith is one which trusts the judgment of the heart, but seeks to understand and develop that judgment with the mind. Mary's faith is proof of St Augustine's dictum that 'faith precedes understanding'. We cannot expect to know God through our reason alone. We know God first and foremost in our hearts from where we can then articulate and develop our knowledge of Him. Knowing God is like knowing a person. It is not like knowing a well-constructed argument. Nobody's description of a person ever matches up to our own meeting with that person. But once we have met them ourselves we can describe them. And so it is with God. Like Mary we must meet God first, and then go on to ponder the outcome of that meeting.

In the example of her own person, Mary can mother us in our faith, gently leading us to a knowledge of God which balances both head and heart. As our guide and pattern, she can keep us from the anxieties of a faith which is too tied to reason, or the enthusiasms of a faith which is too driven by emotion.

SUMMER'S END

No historical reason can be found for choosing 8 September as Mary's birthday, but the feast comes at an important time in the northern hemisphere because it marks the end of summer. The Feast of the Nativity of the Blessed Virgin Mary is the last of the great and extravagant summer festivals in the Christian calendar. In France, Mary is often known as 'Our Lady of the Vendange' (grape harvest) because early September is the time to pick the grapes for the new wine and her feast day is the traditional time for the grape harvest festival.

In the mountains of the European Alps, the Feast of Mary is also the time to recognize the end of summer. The 'down-driving' of the herds has traditionally always begun around the Feast of Mary's Nativity when the cattle are led down from their high summer pasture to the valleys below, where stables and hay await them for the winter. Also around the time of this feast, the swallows confirm their reputation as 'Mary's Birds' by leaving central and northern Europe once again and flying south to warmer climes in Africa. Having arrived around the Feast of the Annunciation, they now leave again at the Feast of Mary's Nativity.

TWO OTHER FEASTS OF MARY

Roman Catholics and Orthodox Christians honour Mary in two other great feasts each year. One celebrates her immaculate conception, the other her assumption into heaven. Like the Feast of Mary's Nativity, these feasts are very ancient and concern her person rather than her role. They are not based on events in the gospels but represent instead what Christians have come to believe about Mary over the centuries.

THE IMMACULATE CONCEPTION

8 December is the Feast Day of the Immaculate Conception of the Virgin Mary. Because of her extraordinary position as Christ's mother, Christians felt very early on that Mary must have been an exceptionally pure and holy person. How else could she have conceived, and carried within her, the saviour of the world? They therefore believed that Mary herself must have been born without sin, in other words that she was conceived immaculately.

From the seventh century onwards this belief and its feast day became increasingly popular and spread from Jerusalem to the whole of western Europe and beyond. In 1854 the Feast of the Immaculate Conception eventually became accepted as one of the highest ranking feasts in the Roman Catholic Church. At the same time, Pope Pius IX also confirmed the belief in Mary's immaculate conception as a dogma of the Roman Church.

THE ASSUMPTION

The Feast of the Assumption remembers Mary's death and is celebrated on 15 August. It dates back to the sixth century and was made an official feast day by Emperor Maurititius in AD 602. It was originally called the Feast of the Falling Asleep of the Mother of God, or the Dormition. Today it is still called by this name in the Orthodox Church but is known as the Feast of the Assumption in the Roman Catholic Church, from the Latin word *assumptio* which means to take up.

The feast commemorates the belief that the Virgin Mary did not die and that her body did not decay. Instead, she fell asleep, and while her soul ascended to heaven, her body was also carried there to be with Christ. In heaven her body and soul were reunited and she was crowned as the Queen of Heaven. The feast therefore celebrates these three things: Mary's falling asleep; her assumption into heaven; and her coronation. Like the Immaculate Conception, this feast has been an extremely popular one in the Roman Catholic Church for many centuries, but belief in Mary's assumption into heaven was only made an official dogma by Pope Pius XII in 1950.

The Feast of the Assumption is famous for its processions. One of the best known is one in Italy where statues of Mary and Christ are carried to meet each other in the town centre where they bow to each other three times. The statue of Christ then escorts the statue of his mother back to the church and in through the church doors as if they were the gates of heaven.

OUR LADY'S THIRTY DAYS

The thirty days between 15 August and 15 September are known as Our Lady's Thirty Days. These days are believed to be a particularly blessed time of year when all fruit and food produced is said to be particularly tasty and all water especially healthy and invigorating. A swim on the Feast of the Assumption, or in the 30 days thereafter, is meant to keep you healthy for the whole of the next year. Mary is particularly associated with herbs and their medicinal powers. August is the time to pick many herbs in Europe, and the Feast of the Assumption is a traditional time to bless all herbs and pray for their healing power in the months ahead. The feast is also the time to bless orchards, animals, fields and fishing boats.

READINGS

Luke 1:39–49 and 2:1–19

A PRAYER FOR THE BLESSED VIRGIN MARY

O my Lady, the Holy Virgin Mary, thou hast been likened to many things, yet there is nothing which compares with thee. Neither heaven can match thee, nor the earth equal as much as the measure of thy womb. For thou didst confine the Unconfineable, and carry him whom none has power to sustain.

Honour to her who bore thee; homage to her who gave birth to thee; devotion to thy mother; and holiness to her who tended thee.

From the Hymn to the Blessed Virgin, Ethiopian Orthodox Church, in *The Oxford Book of Prayer*

Harvest Festival and Thanksgiving

While the earth lasts, seedtime and harvest, cold and heat,
summer and winter, day and night, shall never cease.
Genesis 8:22

Festivals of thanksgiving for the harvest are as old as humanity. Every religion gives thanks to God for the harvest and prays for renewed blessings on the land for each new cropping season. But harvest times differ around the world so there is no fixed date for a harvest festival in the Christian calendar. Different peoples celebrate the harvest at the different times of the year when they have gathered it in.

THANKSGIVING

In the USA, the fourth Thursday in November is a national holiday when people give thanks for the harvest and feast on the famous dishes of turkey, cranberry sauce, sweet potato and pumpkin pie. This custom dates back to a thanksgiving celebration for the first ever harvest gathered in by the original European settlers to New England, the so-called Pilgrim Fathers. In 1621 they shared a three-day festival of harvest thanksgiving with their American Indian neighbours amongst whom they had settled and who had helped them with their first crop. The Indians had taught these Europeans how to cultivate sweetcorn, pumpkin, sweet potatoes and cranberries, and had also shown them how to catch wild turkey. This annual Thanksgiving feast was practised widely for centuries in the USA until finally, in 1863, President Abraham Lincoln made Thanksgiving a national holiday.

The early settlers had probably brought the idea of a three-day harvest festival from their own Christian communities in Europe. In France, for example, it has always been the custom to celebrate the harvest at Martinmas (St Martin's Day) on 11 November, by which time the crops are gathered and the first of the new wine from the September grape harvest could be sampled. The centrepiece of this feast was roast goose – known as 'Martin's Goose'.

THE WILD HARVEST

At Harvest Festival we do not just give thanks for what people have cultivated. We also give thanks for those things which grow wild and which appear every year of their own accord. Harvest festivals often take place when wild fruits like berries are at their peak in the hedgerows or when the woods and fields are covered with wild mushrooms. In northern Europe, harvest festivals often coincide with the ripening of wild chestnuts which are delicious and warming to eat roasted over an open fire, and horse chestnuts which provide children (and sometimes their parents!) with hours of fun when played with as conkers. Harvest festival is also the time to remember the harvest of the seas and the rivers and to give thanks for fish and seafood. September harvest festivals can also celebrate the return of a month with an 'r' in its spelling – the time to eat oysters once again!

A SPECIAL CHURCH SERVICE

Churches are never more splendidly decorated than they are at Harvest Festival. As so often happens in Christian festivals, it is children who take the lead in the preparations and celebrations for Harvest Festival. All kinds of fruit, vegetables and crops are brought into the church and children help to display them around the altar, the pews and the window sills. Every household tries to bring something as a mark of thanks to God for the harvest. But all this food is not simply for display and is not just an offering to God. After the service children distribute everything on display as gifts to the poor, the sick or the elderly in the parish.

A GREEN FESTIVAL FOR URBAN COMMUNITIES

Today, the great majority of people in industrialized societies live in towns or cities. Most of us have very few links with the countryside and know little about farming and the workings of the agricultural calendar. Much of our food is processed and packaged for us and few of us have ever worked the land. Cropping seasons mean little to us because, if we have the money, we can usually buy imported fruit and vegetables which are not in season in our own countries. So, for example, we can eat apples and oranges all year round.

Just because we are not farmers does not mean that we cannot celebrate the harvest. Indeed, a harvest festival has a particularly important place in the Christian calendar for urban communities. It reminds us of our ultimate dependence on the earth and its cultivation, and of our obligations to the natural world. Harvest Festival is a time to focus on the environment which sustains our food supply. It lets us give God thanks for that environment and, equally important, it lets us think about how our industrial societies use and abuse that environment.

In the northern hemisphere, the main harvest usually falls in the season of ordinary time which follows Pentecost when the liturgical colour is green. It makes good sense to celebrate Harvest Festival as a green festival with all the new ecological and environmental meanings of that colour. The resounding message to come from the green movement is that we all have an impact on the natural world. The actions of each one of us, as consumer or producer, are a link in a longer chain of action which can either protect or destroy our natural environment. The choice is ours.

SUSTAINING FUTURE HARVESTS

God put mankind in the Garden of Eden 'to till it and keep it' (Genesis 2:15). With our increasing technology we are able to till the earth more than ever before. But this same technology also puts us at risk, as never before, of being unable to keep the earth and its resources in the condition in which we have inherited it from previous generations. Harvest Festivals, while giving us the chance to thank God for the riches of the natural world, also present us with the more solemn task of contemplating our responsibilities to nature. In more and more Harvest Festival services today, the thanks which Christians give to God is uttered alongside promises to keep and sustain our environment, which is, after all, the means of all future harvests.

HARVEST PRAYERS

God stir the soil,
Run the ploughshare deep,
Cut the furrows round and round,
Overturn the hard, dry ground,
Spare no strength nor toil,
Even though I weep.
In the loose, fresh mangled earth
Sow new seed.
Free of withered vine and weed
Bring fair flowers to birth.

A Prayer from Singapore, in *The Lion Prayer Collection*

The seed is Christ's,
The granary is Christ's;
In the granary of God
May we be gathered.
The sea is Christ's,
The fishes are Christ's;
In the nets of God
May we all meet.

Irish Prayer, in *The Lion Prayer Collection*

Hallowtide

The last day of October marks the beginning of the three-day period known as Hallowtide when Christians remember the dead. These three days involve All-Hallows Eve, or Hallowe'en, on 31 October, All Saints' Day on 1 November and All Souls' Day on 2 November. The word 'hallow' is an old English word meaning to 'make holy' and All-Hallows refers to all the saints – the holy ones.

The Christian Church has always recognized both the living and the dead among its members. Hallowtide is an important time to reaffirm this truth. All-Hallows Eve, All Saints and All Souls are festivals which recognize and cherish the memory of those who have gone before us: those we never knew, as well as those we knew and loved. In celebrating their memory we can come to know, and be glad, that with us they share in Christ's eternal kingdom.

All-Hallows Eve

31 October is All-Hallows Eve, or Hallowe'en. The night before All Saints' Day, Hallowe'en has come to absorb many of the ancient pre-Christian rites from this time of year which were associated with the return of winter and the spirits of the dead. In the ancient societies of Europe, the dark months of winter were believed to be the season of evil spirits. Early November, therefore, marked the season when these spirits came into their own once more and roamed the earth in strength, delighted at the weakening powers of the sun.

DARK DAYS

For many centuries therefore, early November was the time for people to explore the dark side of life. Burning barrels were carried through towns and villages and hurled into rivers and lakes to imitate the failing of the sun. Great bonfires were lit to encourage that same sun and as a warning to dark spirits who were burnt in effigy. In Britain today, Bonfire Night on 5 November is a relic of these pre-Christian winter festivals which received new meaning after Guy Fawkes' plot to burn down Parliament. On 5 November 1605, Guy Fawkes was discovered in the basement of the Parliament building in London, gunpowder in hand. Since then, winter bonfires have made this particular political traitor the villain in their ritual instead of more sinister spiritual demons.

DEVILISH GAMES

Hallowe'en still keeps many of the old pre-Christian games and rituals as part of its festivities. Games involving apples, dressing up and retribution are still enjoyed by children every Hallowe'en. In ancient Rome, the feast of Pomona, the Goddess of Gardens and Orchards, was celebrated on 1 November and many of today's apple games may stem from ancient celebrations in her honour. Apples were a sacred fruit to the ancient Celts as well. The most well known apple game is 'bobbing for apples' in a bucket of water with your hands behind your back and only being allowed to catch them in your mouth. Another similar game is 'snapping for apples', when apples are hung by their stalks from a tree and must be caught with the mouth. Many of these games are de-signed to create maximum fun with equal measure of humil-iation and triumph. The old traditions maintained that if you succeeded you would have good luck and good health and if you failed, then the year ahead might be a bad one.

Dressing up as witches and ghosts at Hallowe'en also goes back to ancient winter festivals. In winter, it was be-lieved that the evil spirits who were out in force were deter-mined to trick people and do them harm. A cunning form of disguise was reckoned to be the best response to such a threat, and people set out to deceive the demons by masquerading as some kind of evil spirit themselves. The hope was that the real demons would then mistake you as one of their own and leave you alone. Apart from dressing up, Hallowe'en is also a time for spectacularly lurid children's recipes which use dark colours like black, blues and deep reds. Inspired by supposed witches' potions they have names like 'eyeball jelly' and 'worm soup'.

PUMPKINS

Pumpkins come into season in Europe and America around October and also play a major part in Hallowe'en rituals. While the bright yellow flesh of the pumpkin can be scooped out and made into a delicious soup or steaming pie, the hard orange skin is traditionally carved to make a garish pumpkin lantern. Large round pumpkins are cut with triangular eyes and big toothy grins, and inside is placed a candle or light of some kind. The grinning lanterns are then used as decoration for Hallowe'en parties. Before the pumpkin arrived in Europe from America, people used the smaller swedes and turnips for this custom. While more difficult to cut precisely, swedes and turnips are much lighter than pumpkins and so are often hung on a pole and carried as lanterns through the streets. Like masks and fancy dress, pumpkin lanterns were intended to frighten or mislead evil spirits.

The camouflage of fancy dress and pumpkin lanterns also provided the perfect cover under which to get even with an enemy. Hallowe'en therefore became an inevitable and acceptable time to settle old scores through the ancient custom of 'trick or treat', a game which is extremely popular with many children today. Dressed up beyond recognition, people would approach those who had offended them somehow in the previous year. They would then threaten the person with an act of retribution or demand satisfaction for their grievance by a gift of some kind – a trick or a treat. By this custom old scores were settled by payment of money, food or drink, or revenge was exacted by a prank of some kind.

EXPLORING THE DARK SIDE

When enjoyed in a genuinely festive spirit of fun and goodwill, Hallowe'en can be an important time for children in particular to explore the dark side of life. Within the gentle boundaries of games and costumes they can experience their fear of the dark and their images of evil in the safety of make-believe. Such games make Hallowe'en a special night for children when the rules of normal life are suspended. They are free to roam through gardens and dark streets after bedtime, and because of their supposedly terrifying disguise they find themselves in an apparent position of power over adults. Imagining themselves beyond recognition, they can enjoy the privilege of the mask which lets them step out of role and play another part.

It is important that Hallowe'en remains a game and that children's fears and pranks are kept safe within the realms of play. Above all, it is important for children to understand that Hallowtide is not just about Hallowe'en. Part of the excitement of All-Hallows Eve is that it heralds the holy days themselves, the feasts of All Saints and All Souls.

TAKING EVIL SERIOUSLY

But if the celebration of Hallowe'en has its positive side, it also has a dangerous side. Fascination with the occult remains in many societies today and Hallowe'en is often a time for young people in particular to experiment with evil rituals. Lured into such activities by a sense of daring, or misled by books and films about the occult, some young people soon find themselves terrified, disturbed and way out of their depth.

Christianity has a strong belief in the reality of evil in our world. The fun and games of Hallowe'en should not obscure the very real tendency of some to ally themselves with evil and to be distorted by it. Just as every year a small group of people are always injured by fireworks on bonfire night, so too a small group of young people are affected by involvement in the occult. And it is often left to priests and counsellors to pick up the pieces. It is important to draw a clear distinction between party games and sinister ritual and to remember that the real point of Hallowe'en is to turn our minds to those who have triumphed, in Christ, over the powers of death and hell. For the very next day, we come to All Saints' Day.

All Saints' Day

*How blest are those who have suffered persecution
for the cause of right, the kingdom of heaven is theirs.*
Matthew 5:10

All Saints' Day, on 1 November, is the day we remember
those exceptional Christians who died for their faith or who
lived extraordinarily holy lives. The Feast of All Saints dates
back to fifth century Antioch in Syria where the church dedicated a day to the memory of all the Christian martyrs who
had been killed for their faith. Until then, the early Church
had remembered each martyr on a particular day of the
year, but soon there were more martyrs than days in the year
and so a communal feast was held in their honour. It was
also recognized that many martyrs and saints were unknown
and uncelebrated. This feast was for them too. From early in
the fifth century, the feast of All Martyrs was originally held
on Easter Friday by the church at Antioch and on the eighth
day after Pentecost in the rest of the Eastern Church. In the
seventh century, the Roman Church took up the feast using
the more common Eastern date after Pentecost.

Originally, therefore, the saints were honoured and remembered as part of the joyful celebrations of the Easter
cycle. Their special place in heaven was celebrated as part of
the wider celebrations of the resurrection. In the Eastern
Church the saints are still remembered at this time, but in 844
Pope Gregory IV moved All Saints Day to 1 November for the
Western Church. In the northern hemisphere, this turned it
from a bright early summer feast to a dark autumnal feast.

Pope Gregory supposedly had two reasons for the change of date. First, early November was the traditional time for pre-Christian religions in Rome to remember the dead, so celebrations of the dead already took place at this time of year. Secondly, on a more practical level, the November date came soon after the main harvest of the year and so made it easier to feed the many pilgrims who descended on the city for this popular feast. With its gloomy days and falling leaves, early November in the northern hemisphere is an appropriate time to remember death and loss. But such an atmosphere makes it difficult to joyfully celebrate past lives and memories, an important part of Hallowtide which might come more easily at the original timing of the feast in early summer.

A CELEBRATION OF VIRTUE

The original feast of All Martyrs soon came to include remembrance of all the saints. It remembered not only those who were martyred for their faith, but also the saints who were great teachers of the faith, known as confessors, together with simpler saints who had lived exemplary and holy lives.

Through the ages, the lives of the saints and the stories of their heroic and virtuous acts have inspired countless Christians. When few people could read, the lives of the saints were easily remembered as models of Christian virtue. Saints were usually remembered for particularly striking deeds which were supreme examples of Christian virtues such as faith, hope, charity, courage, justice, self-control or good sense. These stories were continually retold and served as parables which encouraged illiterate and learned people alike in the ways of the good life. The symbols of a saint's special deeds are usually depicted in their statues and pictures to prompt people's memory. For example, St Martin of Tours is always represented with his splendid cloak which he cut in half to give to a shivering beggar. St Catherine of Alexandria is shown with a spiked wheel and St Sebastian usually holds an arrow as a reminder of the terrible methods of their respective martyrdoms.

HEAVENLY FRIENDSHIPS

The saints are our ancestors on earth and precede us in heaven. Many Christians experience a strong sense that the saints are still with us, that they watch over us and intercede with God on our behalf. Although dead, they are still members of Christ's Church, and living Christians have often found great comfort in firm friendships with saints long dead who are now at peace in heaven. Many people find that the life of one particular saint speaks to them above others and so have a particular devotion to that saint.

A DAY OF THANKSGIVING

All Saints' Day is a day to give thanks for the lives of the saints and for all they do for us as continuing examples of the good life. In our thanks it is important to remember especially the original theme of martyrdom for which the feast day was first founded. Throughout history and throughout the world today, Christians have suffered, and continue to suffer, for their faith and for the rights of others. While we know and venerate the names of the great saints and the martyrs of our own time, there are many martyrs whose names we do not know. One reason behind the establishment of the original festival was to give thanks for these martyrs whom we cannot remember by name. On this day above all others in the year, we recall them and their deeds, unknown to us but cherished by God and by those whose lives they changed.

READINGS

Revelation 7:2–4, 9
Matthew 5:1–12
Luke 6:20–23

A PRAYER FOR ALL SAINTS

We thank thee, O God, for the saints of all ages; for those who in times of darkness kept the lamp of faith burning; for the great souls who saw visions of larger truth and dared to declare it; for the multitude of quiet and gracious souls whose presence has purified and sanctified the world; and for those known and loved by us, who have passed from this earthly fellowship into the fuller light of life with thee. AMEN

Anon., in *The Oxford Book of Prayer*

All Souls' Day

WHITE, VIOLET OR BLACK

The righteous will be remembered for ever;
the memory of the righteous is a blessing.
Psalm 112:6

2 November is All Souls' Day when we remember and pray for all the dead, especially our loved ones. For the first thousand years of its existence the Church had no special day on which to remember the dead. Until the eleventh century, people would remember their own dead on the particular anniversaries of a person's death. But in 1048, Odilo, the Abbot of the Benedictine monastery at Cluny near Paris, instructed his monks to hold 2 November as a day of remembrance and prayer for 'all the departed'. It soon became obligatory for all Benedictines to celebrate this day and the practice spread rapidly throughout the Western Church until it was made an official feast day of the church in the fourteenth century.

Remembrance of the dead in the Eastern Church developed differently. As with All Saints' Day, the Eastern Church has kept its remembrance of the dead as part of the Easter cycle where it takes place in the three weeks before Lent. It does not celebrate a single All Souls' Day. Instead, the Orthodox Church remembers its dead in three different groups on three separate days. On the third Friday before Lent the Orthodox Church remembers all departed priests. On the second Friday before Lent it remembers all the faithful departed. And finally, on the Friday before Lent it remembers all those who died in strange places away from their family and friends.

MAKING SPACE FOR THE DEAD

Many modern cultures are not good with death. Our busy lives leave little room for it and our customs tend to tidy it away. Even when we are exposed to death we are protected from it by professionals like doctors, undertakers and lawyers. It is possible for a person to go through their entire life in the Western world without seeing a dead body. A fear of death is natural, but a tendency to turn one's back on the dead and the bereaved is neither healthy nor Christian. The dead are part of the Church, and Jesus singled out the bereaved as worthy of special attention and care when he said: 'Blessed are those who mourn for they shall be comforted' (Matthew 5:4).

All Souls' Day, and the whole of Hallowtide, gives us the opportunity to be open about death. It is the one time in the year when the word death need not be uttered in hushed tones. All Souls, in particular, lets us remember our dead and feel our loss. It also allows us to celebrate their past lives and pray for their peace. Above all, it gives us the time to recognize the dead's continuing presence in our lives: in our memories; in our affections, and in their abiding influence upon us.

Christian Hallowtide customs have always encouraged people to celebrate All Souls' Day in a way which recognizes our continuing relationship with the dead. The week before All Souls is a time to visit cemeteries and to tend and decorate the graves of loved ones. Cemetery plots are weeded, mown and covered with fresh flowers. New gravel is laid and tombstones are painted or repaired. In many countries, covered candles will be lit beside the graves and left burning throughout the night on All Saints Eve and All Souls Eve so that the cemeteries are bathed in light and memory of the dead burns bright. On All Souls' Day itself the congregation follows the priest in procession through the cemetery while he blesses it and sprinkles each grave with holy water.

All Souls is also a time of great bell ringing when the sound of the bells reminds people to pray for the dead. In some churches, people will also bring lists of the names of their dead for the priest to read out in services throughout November. Requiem masses are also often sung in honour of the dead at All Souls. The Latin word *requiem* means rest and comes from the first line of this special funeral mass: 'Eternal rest grant unto them'. Many of the great composers including Mozart, Brahms and Fauré have composed settings of this mass. This music captures the unutterable sadness of death but combines it with a serenity that conveys the Christian conviction that death is not the end.

SOUL FOOD

There are a number of old customs about feeding the dead at All Souls. Such customs spring from the belief that the dead are especially close to us at Hallowtide and that we should make them welcome in the places which were once their own. In many parts of Europe 'soul food' was made ready for the departed souls who might return around All Souls. Special breads and bean stews were cooked and feasted on in honour of the dead, and portions were left out for them overnight. Even though the nights were getting colder, windows and doors were left slightly open for them so that they could enter into their old earthly dwellings to eat and make themselves at home again. In some countries, extra places were traditionally laid at supper on All Souls Eve for recently departed relatives so that there was space for them round the family table once again. The next day, on All Souls' Day itself, the extra soul food was given to children and the poor who went 'souling' from door to door, singing songs and asking for something to eat. A wide variety of 'All Souls Bread' and 'All Souls Cake' is therefore common at Hallowtide, with one Spanish pastry having the particularly graphic name of 'Bones of the Holy'.

REMEMBRANCE SUNDAY

This century, early November has also become the time to remember those who have died in war. The armistice which ended the First World War was signed on 11 November 1918. From then on this day was known as Armistice Day and devoted to the memory of the war dead. After the Second World War, Armistice Day became known as

Remembrance Day or Veterans' Day and it remembers all the war dead from this century's conflicts. It is now held on the second Sunday in November, and in Britain it is customary to wear a poppy on Remembrance Sunday. This red wild flower continued to grow on the terrible battlefields of France in World War One and has become the symbol of remembrance. During the service on Remembrance Sunday the famous two minutes silence is held in honour of the dead.

A PRAYER AT ALL SOULS

May he support us all the day long, till the shades lengthen, and the evening comes, and the busy world is hushed, and the fever of life is over, and our work is done! Then in his mercy may he give us a safe lodging, and a holy rest, and peace at the last.

John Henry Newman, in *The Oxford Book of Prayer*

The End of the Year

The Christian Year comes to an end around All Souls' Day on the 23rd, and last, Sunday after Pentecost. The following week, the new sacred year then opens again on the Ninth Sunday before Christmas, the fifth before Advent. With this new year, the slow waiting for the light of the world begins again and the mysteries of Advent, Christmas, Holy Week, Easter and Pentecost unfold once more.

Appendix One
Sunday Themes
Throughout the Year

The following list gives the main theme for reflection on each Sunday of the year as recommended by the Church of England in the Alternative Service Book. Some Sundays have two themes depending on which year the lectionary is following. Your church may have nominated other themes or given a different emphasis to some Sundays. But the principle of giving each Sunday a particular theme inspired by the gospel readings is a good one. It helps to add structure and meaning to our passage through the Christian Year, and gives a pattern to our thinking and our praying.

9th before Christmas	The Creation
8th before Christmas	The Fall
7th before Christmas	The Election of God's People: Abraham
6th before Christmas	The Promise of Redemption: Moses
5th before Christmas	The Remnant of Israel
1st in Advent	The Advent Hope
2nd in Advent	The Word of God in the Old Testament
3rd in Advent	The Forerunner

4th in Advent	The Annunciation
1st after Christmas	The Incarnation/The Presentation
2nd after Christmas	The Holy Family/The Light of the World
1st after Epiphany	Revelation: The Baptism of Christ
2nd after Epiphany	Revelation: The First Disciples
3rd after Epiphany	Revelation: Signs of Glory
4th after Epiphany	Revelation: The New Temple
5th after Epiphany	Revelation: The Wisdom of God
6th after Epiphany	Revelation: Parables
9th before Easter	Christ the Teacher
8th before Easter	Christ the Healer
7th before Easter	Christ the Friend of Sinners
1st in Lent	The King and the Kingdom: Temptation
2nd in Lent	The King and the Kingdom: Conflict
3rd in Lent	The King and the Kingdom: Suffering
4th in Lent	The King and the Kingdom: Transfiguration
5th in Lent	The King and the Kingdom: Victory of the Cross
Palm Sunday	The Way of the Cross

Easter Day	
1st after Easter	The Upper Room/The Bread of Life
2nd after Easter	The Emmaus Road/The Good Shepherd
3rd after Easter	The Lakeside/The Resurrection and the Life
4th after Easter	The Charge to Peter/The Way, the Truth, and the Life
5th after Easter	Going to the Father
After Ascension Day	The Ascension of Christ
Pentecost	
Trinity Sunday	
2nd after Pentecost	The People of God/The Church's Unity and Fellowship
3rd after Pentecost	The Life of the Baptized/The Church's Confidence in Christ
4th after Pentecost	The Freedom of the Sons of God/The Church's Mission to the Individual
5th after Pentecost	The New Law/The Church's Mission to All Men
6th after Pentecost	The New Man
7th after Pentecost	The More Excellent Way
8th after Pentecost	The Fruit of the Spirit
9th after Pentecost	The Whole Armour of God
10th after Pentecost	The Mind of Christ
11th after Pentecost	The Serving Community
12th after Pentecost	The Witnessing Community

13th after Pentecost	The Suffering Community
14th after Pentecost	The Family
15th after Pentecost	Those in Authority
16th after Pentecost	The Neighbour
17th after Pentecost	The Proof of Faith
18th after Pentecost	The Offering of Life
19th after Pentecost	The Life of Faith
20th after Pentecost	Endurance
21st after Pentecost	The Christian Hope
22nd after Pentecost	The Two Ways
Last after Pentecost	Citizens of Heaven

Appendix Two
A List of Saints' Days

The following list gives the dates of some of the Saints' Days celebrated throughout the Christian Church. The list is obviously a small one, concentrating on Apostles and British saints.

There are many thousands of other saints remembered and revered by Christians throughout the world, some of whom may have particular importance to you. They may be local saints intimately connected with the place where you live. They may be the patron saint of the kind of work you do. Or they may be people who lived a life of faith which is particularly resonant of your own ideals or your own personal experience. Whatever the connection, remembering the lives of special saints on particular days of the year is an important means of deepening our faith.

JANUARY

17th	Anthony of Egypt (AD 356)
21st	Agnes of Rome (AD 304)
25th	The Conversion of St Paul
28th	Thomas Aquinas (AD 1274)

FEBRUARY

3rd   Saints and Martyrs of Europe
21st   Saints and Martyrs of Africa

MARCH

1st   David, Patron Saint of Wales (AD 601)
7th   Perpetua and her companions (AD 203)
17th   Patrick, Patron Saint of Ireland (AD 460)
19th   Joseph of Nazareth, husband of the Blessed
      Virgin Mary
20th   Cuthbert, Bishop of Lindisfarne (AD 687)

APRIL

8th   Saints and Martyrs of the Americas
23rd   George, Patron Saint of England
25th   Mark the Evangelist
29th   Catherine of Siena

MAY

1st   Philip and James, Apostles
2nd   Athanasius of Alexandria (AD 373)
8th   Julian of Norwich (AD 1417)
14th   Matthias, Apostle
26th   Augustine of Canterbury (AD 605)

JUNE

 9th   Columba of Iona (AD 597)
11th   Barnabas, Apostle
14th   Fathers of the Eastern Church
22nd Alban, first British Martyr (AD 209)
24th   John the Baptist
29th   Peter, Apostle

JULY

 3rd   Thomas, Apostle
 6th   Thomas More (AD 1535)
11th   Benedict, Abbot (AD 550)
22nd Mary Magdalene
25th   James, Apostle
26th   Anne, Mother of the Blessed Virgin Mary

AUGUST

 4th   Dominic, Friar (AD 1221)
11th   Clare of Assisi (AD 1253)
24th   Bartholomew, Apostle
28th   Augustine of Hippo (AD 430)
31st   Aidan of Lindisfarne (AD 651)

SEPTEMBER

20th   Saints and Martyrs of Australia and the Pacific
21st   Matthew, Apostle
29th   Michael and All Angels

OCTOBER

4th   Francis of Assisi
13th   Edward the Confessor
15th   Teresa of Avila
18th   Luke, Apostle
28th   Simon and Jude, Apostles

NOVEMBER

8th   Saints and Martyrs of England
11th   Martin of Tours (AD 397)
17th   Hilda of Whitby (AD 680)
30th   Andrew, Apostle and Patron Saint of Scotland

DECEMBER

3rd   Saints and Martyrs of Asia
14th   John of the Cross (AD 1591)
26th   Stephen, the first Martyr
27th   John, Evangelist
29th   Thomas Becket of Canterbury (AD 1170)